WHATEVER HAPPENED TO ORDINARY CHRISTIANS?

JIM SMOKE

HARVEST HOUSE PUBLISHERS
Eugene, Oregon 97402

WHATEVER HAPPENED TO ORDINARY CHRISTIANS?

Eugene, Oregon 97402

Library of Congress Catalog Card Number 87-081666
ISBN 0-89081-605-0

Printed in the United States of America.

Dedicated to

Jack and Marijean Hamilton,

our friends

. . . two remarkably ordinary Christians who have lived extraordinary lives filled with gentle wisdom, quiet guidance, and persistent affirmation!

Contents

I Want to Be an Ordinary Christian!

Introduction

I Want to Be an Ordinary Christian!

That's why I am writing this book. It is as much for me as it is for you. Perhaps it is even more for me because, if I can get a good handle on it, I can better help you get a firmer grasp.

You are probably already asking the question, "In the age of the sensational, the superb, and the extraordinary, who in their right mind wants to be ordinary?" Ordinary is vanilla when everyone wants pistachio. Ordinary is plain wrap when everyone wants fancy. Ordinary is average when everyone wants to be above average. Ordinary is being in the line when everyone wants to be at the head of the line. Ordinary is not attracting attention when everyone wants attention. Ordinary is simply not "IN."

In the secular world, and increasingly in the Christian world, acclaim, fame, and attention go to those who seemingly have transcended the ordinary and are rewarded publicly for their conquests. I have yet to see an award presented to anyone for being ordinary. Ordinary people do not sit at head tables. Ordinary people do not attract attention.

There are really only two kinds of people around us today: those who are ordinary and those who don't want to be. There are probably two kinds of Christians also: those who are ordinary Christians and those who don't want to be (ordinary, that is; not Christian).

Probably for the first time in history, we have created within the Christian community our very own Christian star system. Christian "stars" are people who have been elevated above the ordinary by their extraordinary accomplishments. We tend to rate Christian personalities like restaurants. The top ones get a five-star rating (they're invited to the biggest and best Christian confabs). The four-stars receive second-level invitations (with the chance to appear in megachurches). The three-stars get to debut at denominational conclaves. The two-stars appear at churches with less than five hundred members. The one-stars are spending their time polishing their newly acquired stars and wondering how to fill their calendars.

It is easy to spend our time stargazing, starworshiping, starshopping, and starfollowing. It is also becoming very easy to let the extraordinary Christian stars do the ministry that all ordinary Christians were called by Christ to do.

The plea and purpose of this book is twofold: first, to disentangle the ordinary Christian from the star system and, second, to grapple realistically with how ordinary Christians are supposed to live and follow Christ.

In Acts 17:6 we read the simple account of a handful of ordinary Christians of whom it was said, "These men who have upset the world have come here also" (NASB). It is a tragedy that we have taken the call to be "upsetters" away from ordinary Christians today and placed it on a select few whose only word to the ordinary Christian is, "Send your gifts this week."

The call to be an ordinary Christian is the call to be a servant Christian. Service is seldom performed well in isolation. It is performed best in community. This book is about building ordinary Christians in community and life with one another. Perhaps after reading it, you will want to be an ordinary Christian too!

A special thanks to Ed Stewart for his editorial expertise in working with this manuscript.

Jim Smoke
Tempe, Arizona
1987

Has Anybody Seen an Ordinary Christian?

1

Has Anybody Seen an Ordinary Christian?

OR-DI-NARY. . . . "of common or everyday occurrence: customary, usual, according to an established order, regular, normal."

CHRIS-TIAN. . . . "manifesting the spirit of Christ or His teachings. A disciple of Jesus of Nazareth; one whose profession and life conform to the example and teachings of Jesus."

A wise person once said, "If you are going to mean what you say, find out the meaning of what you are saying." If I want to be an ordinary Christian, I need to know the meaning of those two words. The definitions above, from my single-volume, super-thick dictionary, help me reach my objective. As I look at the definition of the word "ordinary," I get a good, secure, comfortable feeling from the synonyms "regular" and "normal." When someone tells me I am normal, I feel a lot better than I do if someone tells me I am abnormal. This definition of "ordinary" gives me a feeling of acceptability, belonging, order.

Yet if I feel comfortable with the word, why do I constantly try to climb above its confines and seek the label "extraordinary"? Probably because the society in which I live, both secular and sacred, urges me upward to the next rung. The problem with climbing the ladder stretching above ordinariness is that there is always another rung above. And soon the endless rungs become the only thing by which we measure ourselves.

It was said that Alexander the Great cried one day because he had no more worlds to conquer. Perhaps it's harder to go down the ladder than up.

Ordinary Is Okay

Ordinary, although comfortable and acceptable in many ways, does not seem to be a place where we want to unpack and settle down. Instead, it's a place we'd rather escape from at the earliest possible moment. Even though we all live perhaps most of our time in the valley of the ordinary, we all appear determined to move higher at the first opportunity. The knowledge that God uses ordinary Christians today doesn't seem to have any effect on our residency. Most of us feel that God is using everyone else more effectively than He is using us. (And we know without a doubt that He is using the Christian superstars more strategically than the nonstars!)

Even Paul's words in 1 Corinthians 1:27–29 don't impact us much: "But God has chosen the foolish things of the world to shame the wise, and God has chosen the weak things of the world to shame the things which are strong, and the base things of the world and the despised, God has chosen, the things that are not, that He might nullify the things that are, that no man should boast before God" (NASB). Simply insert the word "ordinary" for the words "foolish," "weak," and "base." If you are still unconvinced that God specializes in using ordinary people, then you have read too many books dealing with how to be successful and above average.

Scripture consistently verifies that God used ordinary things and ordinary people to achieve extraordinary results. The results, however, were never intended to elevate the person. The results were always to bring glory to God, not a person. One of the reasons many Christian leaders today struggle with their accomplishments is that they allow themselves to be elevated instead of God. Some would even rewrite the old song, "To God be the glory, great things He hath done—but He knows He couldn't have done it without me!" As someone has said, you only get in trouble when you start believing your own press releases.

It is relatively easy to sit in the worship service on Sunday and believe that God is using the pastor, choir director, musicians, and even ushers more than He is using you or me. Many of us feel that the way to be used of God and be delivered from the ordinary is to stand in front of a group. God *must* use you if you are standing up front, right? I don't think so. I have been standing up front many times when I think God would rather have had me sit down. And sometimes when I sit down, I wish that I had sat down much sooner.

A Christian Is a Conformed Disciple

Coupled with the word "ordinary" is the word "Christian," as you no doubt noticed on the cover of this book. Definitely speaking, we probably wrestle more with the second word than the first. We may try to escape the ordinary for a higher plateau. But we accept the label "Christian" because we decided to follow Christ and give Him our lives, and upon that decision we became Christians. We do not want to escape the title, just the responsibility attached to it.

Your dictionary may define the word "Christian" differently than mine, but the second part of the definition is pretty universal, I would think: "A disciple of Jesus of Nazareth; one whose profession and life conform to the example and teachings of Jesus." I can hear some of you saying, "I like the disciple part, but that part about conformity worries me." Well, it makes me nervous, too. I like being identified as Christ's disciple. But do I conform to Christ's teachings in profession and life? That's the question we will wrestle with throughout this book. What does it really mean to be an ordinary Christian and just what do ordinary Christians do anyway? Are they mere performers in the name of Christ who jump through hoops held high by others' expectations? Or are they real people seeking together to follow Christ's scriptural example in the last years of the twentieth century?

A Vanishing Species

As we identify ordinary Christians in the following pages and examine how they live, we may become acutely aware that they are a vanishing species, much like the California condor where I live. Only a few condors remain in the wild and not many more exist in captivity. Condors in captivity are dying off without reproducing while those in the wild are being killed thoughtlessly by those who don't appreciate their presence any longer. Such may well be the fate of the ordinary Christian—not surviving captivity in the Christian community and slowly being extinguished by those outside the Christian community.

I'm always searching for ordinary Christians as I travel the country. But it seems that whenever I find one, he or she reaches for an upper rung and moves away from me. And I'm striving to be an ordinary Christian in my own spiritual pilgrimage. But in my striving I find little help and a lot of isolation.

Shall I abandon my quest for ordinary Christians or my struggle to become one? Never! I will continue my search for the ordinary Christian in you so that I can share the ordinary Christian in me.

God Loves You Even When You're Limping

2

God Loves You Even When You're Limping

Most all of us have suffered from a limp at one time or another. We twist an ankle, bang a shin, pull a hamstring muscle, or stub a toe and—ouch!—end up hobbling along with a "hitch in our getalong" until it heals. Not only is a leg injury painful, but it nearly always inhibits our ability to get around and often slows down those traveling with us. It's no fun being a limper.

Unfortunately, there are people among us whose ability to walk has been permanently impaired through injury or illness. Increased public awareness of the problems of the handicapped has resulted in better facilities, increasing the mobility of those on crutches or in wheelchairs. And great advances in medical science swell the hope of those who await cures for debilitating illnesses. We can only hope that those who cannot walk now may someday be able to do so.

People ask nosey questions of limpers. What happened to you? How serious is it? How long will you be that way? They seldom ask how they can help out during those limping days. People really don't understand much about limping—until they become limpers themselves.

Welcome to Limpers Anonymous

Did you know that ordinary Christians limp every now and then? I'm not talking about limping because of a physical impairment. I am talking about limping in the soul, spirit, and emotions. The problem with the inward limp is that it can go undetected for months, years, and even a lifetime. You can cover it up so neatly with a quick smile and a few well chosen words in the right place. And no one will ever know that you are injured or ill on the inside.

When you do finally crank up the courage to tell someone about an inner disability, you run the risk of receiving a far from understanding response. Well-meaning Christian friends may simply tell you to be more spiritual or to go hear a speaker address your hurt in a public forum. And being unable to find a sympathetic ear, you decide never to talk about your limp to another person as long as you live.

I seem to meet a lot of limpers in my travels. I am not sure why. Perhaps they see my radar which scans the people I meet for inner hurts and limps. I have discovered that the limpers in the soul and spirit I meet are looking for an understanding person to share with instead of 87 ways to join the nonlimpers of the world. They want to risk coming out of hiding, and they want to know that limping is a normal growth process all of us experience at different times. Some are even asking, "Is it safe for me to limp around you?"

My pastor has a habit of welcoming people to our church on Sunday morning by saying, "Welcome to the local chapter of Sinners Anonymous." Our good Presbyterian folk don't seem to be bothered a whole lot by that. I guess they know that they are sinners. But I wonder what would happen some Sunday if they were all welcomed to "Limpers Anonymous" and told that they could limp "out loud" in our church. They all looked pretty healthy last Sunday. None appeared to be limping in soul or spirit. But I would bet you three of our Sunday bulletins that many were—and still are.

How's It Going—Really?

The trite and often repeated greeting in the Christian community, "How's it going?" is seldom answered with openness and honesty. Even when hurting inside we protect ourselves by answering "Fine!" because we know we won't really be heard if we are truthful or because we know that few folks are willing to bear our revealed burdens.

I have only worked on one church staff in 28 years of ministry where I felt the question "How are you doing?" merited an honest answer because care would be forthcoming if needed. There is an assumption among those of us on the professional side of Christian ministry that we ministers have a corner on wholeness and that limping only occurs among the laity. A friend recently remarked that during his 20 plus years with a Christian organization he was seldom afforded an opportunity to express his inner struggles and need for personal caring.

We seem to fly along in the Christian community on the airline of assumption. Since all looks fine on the exterior, the interior must be fine as well. I'm not suggesting that all Christians are secretly limping in the spirit every day. We must, however, give opportunity to those in our fellowship to share their inner struggles and conflicts in safety and confidence.

I have personally found that people are helped more when I share my own struggles than when I spend all my time telling them how I live above and beyond their struggles. Writing to the Corinthian Church, Paul states, "Therefore I take pleasure in infirmities, in reproaches, in needs, in persecutions, in distresses for Christ's sake. For when I am weak, then I am strong" (2 Corinthians 12:10). Both inner and outer weakness and struggles can be used by the Lord to bring growth to our lives. Yet seldom do we ask the question when invaded by an inner turmoil, "How can God use this thing in my life to help me grow in His grace and love?" Rather, since we live in the age of the quick fix solution, we want to resolve instantly any impediments to our human journey. Many Christian teachers even intimate that our lives will be trouble free if we will only follow the formulas they teach. Numerous Christian books supply countless lists of methods and rules to follow by which we are supposed to reach the state of spiritual utopia where we will never limp again. But as I study my Bible, I find the line of limpers is a lot longer than the line of nonlimpers. True, there is a strong human appeal to find the right formula to dissolve immediately our hurts and struggles. But we will do better to bring our why, how, where, and when questions to the Lord for processing rather than instant resolving.

Have you found yourself in a worship service, Bible study, prayer meeting, Christian conference, or retreat listening to the nice Christian words coming from speakers, musicians, and assorted attendees? Right in the middle of it all, you want to scream out loud, "Stop! This is all well and good and affirming and challenging. But I am hurting in my spirit right now and just need to be loved up close, prayed for, and helped in some practical way by my brothers and sisters and my heavenly Father." I have a strong feeling that every reader of this book has felt that way a few hundred times and seldom, if ever, verbalized it. After all, who wants to wreck a good meeting? We have become so used to Christian performances that we learn to perform right along with everyone else. And so we limp off after the last song and sit alone under a pine tree or in the coffee shop. And when someone asks, "How was the meeting?," we respond with the words, "A real blessing!"—whatever that means.

Limping Out Loud

There seem to be few opportunities in the Christian community for us to express the truth that we limp from time to time and need help and support from others. I know that my own personal pride and tendency for privacy often prohibit me from sharing inner struggles. My sense of self-sufficiency keeps me from limping out loud. I have this pioneer spirit inside me that says, "It's your problem and you can take care of it. You don't need input or help from others."

My spiritual side also gets into the battle persuading me that it is "just God and me" and we don't need anyone else. I realize that beginning with "God and me" is a good starting point. But somewhere along the way we might need to bring a few of our Christian brothers and sisters on board and let them use their unique gifts to help in our healing and growing. It is both a mark of humility and strength to ask for help. We must bear some of the responsibility for personal inner healing ourselves. We cannot always fault others for their lack of caring when we keep the door to our spirit barred by refusing to call for help.

There are always some people around who specialize in limping to get attention. They don't want to get well because they feed on the care and concern of others. I am reminded of the question Jesus asked the man by the pool of Bethesda: "Do you wish to get well?" (John 5:6, NASB). It was not a silly question. Staying sick can have its own special rewards. Beware of those who are making a Christian career out of limping!

First Aid for Limpers

We could list pages of things that cause us to limp in our inner spirits. Some of the things are self-inflicted and some are other-inflicted. Injuries from within or without tend to leave us with our share of inner scar tissue. Rather than identifying all the causes, let me share some things that can help immensely in the healing.

Limping goes with the territory. There is no escape clause in the contract of Christian commitment for impairments to the spirit. Periodic injuries to the inner self are natural and normal. Following Christ does not put us on another planet. We follow Him through the side streets and alleys and malls and churches of this world. We follow Him through the congested pathways of human relationships and experiences. We share in many of the same conflicts and struggles that He experienced as He walked this earth. He not only healed the limpers around Him, but He felt comfortable in their presence. In fact, He welcomed them and in no way made them feel odd or inferior.

When you are not limping, reach out to someone who is. There are days when we feel that we have cleared all the major hurdles from our own personal limper's obstacle course. We are spiritually strong and wish everyone else could be also. At that moment, we might have very little patience with someone who comes alongside us feeling discouraged, distraught, or beaten down. We might even feel that if we try to help them we'll catch what they have and plunge ourselves into the same despair. The Christian journey is most exciting when it is shared and we have been called to involvement. Writing to the early Christians at Galatia, Paul states, "Bear one another's burdens, and thus fulfill the law of Christ" (Galatians 6:2, NASB). Remember that the law of Christ is the law of love. Love isn't love until you give it away!

Checkout what the Bible says. Christians believe that the Bible is the Word of God and that it contains answers for life's many problems. Yet many of us would confess to looking there last for solutions. We tend to run to the Christian bookstore for our answers or to collect assorted bits of advice from our friends. (Yes, both of these resources can be helpful in due course.) I am always amazed when I appear on radio and television talk shows (not my favorite pastime) by how many people call in to collect whatever answers we seem to be dispensing at that particular moment. I am aware that my input can also be helpful to people sometimes, but I always have this nagging question inside: "Have you really checked out what Scripture says about this?"

Most off-the-cuff solutions are merely spiritual Band-Aids hastily applied to the struggles of those around us. Can we really carefully assess what is making us limp at any time and patiently pursue a Scriptural solution? Can we give God time to act through and in that process? Can we receive the promise of strength and guidance that the Word offers? Since the causes of our limping are often intricate and complex, the answers may not come as quickly as we like. Few of us are good waiters, yet the Scripture tells us repeatedly to wait before the Lord. I would venture to say that our answers will come in proportion to our waiting. No waiting, no answers.

I believe that one of the main reasons we develop inner limps is that we have simply run out of strength. The everyday pressures of life have a way of sapping our energy. Everyone seems to be taking courses on how to alleviate stress, yet the affliction appears to be gaining ground. Stress is caused by running out of strength and strengthlessness is caused by not knowing where the real source of our strength is. For the person who does not know God intimately, strength appears to lie in power, money, and success. Tragically, many Christians are beginning to believe the same error.

Strength for the Christian is revealed in the words of the prophet Isaiah: "Those who wait for the LORD will gain new strength; they will mount up with wings like eagles, they will run and not get tired, they will walk and not become weary" (Isaiah 40:31, NASB). There are a lot of tired Christians limping around today who have forgotten the real source of their strength. Notice that the prophet does not say that the Lord promises success. He promises strength. When strength returns, limping abates.

Talking to God about limping. Talking to God about things that cause us to limp is not always easy. Often we must admit that we have caused our own impairment. Confession, repentance, and forgiveness become the process and prerequisite to healing. We don't always deal well with those processes because they make us all very vulnerable.

We are very used to wrapping things up in neat packages in our world. Confession, repentance, and forgiveness often come with aching barrages of tears and blubbering words, both to God and to those around us. Emotions make people feel uncomfortable, and even Christians like to escape the uncomfortable. Perhaps this is why the tearful altar call has vanished from many of our churches. You can cry in your car or at home. Just don't embarrass anyone by doing it in front of our church on Sunday morning. After all, we don't want to be known as an emotional group!

I believe that there are times for private prayer and times for public prayer. We need both to be strong in our walk with God. Occasions of public prayer give our brothers and sisters the opportunity to minister to us and with us in prayer. We will talk more about this area in a later chapter.

Talking to God about limping is allowing God to be at the center of your struggle rather than on the edges looking on. When your strength is renewed, you will know where it came from.

Forgive those who injure you. When others cause us to limp, we must deal with their humanness through God's framework of forgiveness. Forgiveness is the only thing that can rebuild broken relationships. And even then it is seldom easy. In the midst of teaching the disciples to pray, Jesus said, "And forgive us our debts, as we also have forgiven our debtors" (Matthew 6:12). Many people build emotional debts with us through misunderstanding, unkindness, carelessness, and indifference. We are called to administer the oil of forgiveness to others if we are to heal the limping brought into our lives by the actions of others. And let me say here that injurious words and actions do not come exclusively from those who have no relationship with God. The Christian army is often guilty of wounding its own members.

That wounding often comes from our best Christian friends who feel that they are responsible to put us in our spiritual place for the Lord. In reality they may be acting out of their own jealousy, misunderstanding, misinformation, or personal pride. Our churches are littered with wounded Christians put in that condition by well-meaning but spiritually immature friends.

Keep alert for fellow limpers. How do you find fellow limpers who can share your struggles and concerns? You won't find them wearing sweatshirts marked "FELLOW LIMPER." You won't always find them around your church. You may not find very many in your own family. You see, fellow limpers need to have a deep sense of spiritual understanding and that quality is increasingly hard to find. Spiritual understanding usually comes from people who are our spiritual friends. (We will say more about that in a later chapter.) They are usually people who don't talk a lot but who listen keenly, pray lovingly, and smile affirmatively. They may not have had all the limps, lumps, and bruises that we have had, but they have spiritual insight that comes from the heart. Let's go find 50 people like that right now and pass them around! How about just one or two? If you have found one or two, you are most fortunate. They are hard to find but well worth the search. You will always know when you have found one!

Living with Limping

Limping is neither a sign of weakness nor strength. It is the result of imperfect people living in an imperfect world and harrassed by a sinful nature. It is not something to make a cause for or find a cure from. It is not caused by some kind of spiritual imperfection or flying fungus. It just goes with the territory.

We will be subject to injuries of the soul and spirit throughout our earthly journey and will only be really free from them when we stand before God and begin to spend eternity in His presence.

In the meantime, there is a place at the table of the Lord for those who limp even as there was a place at the table of

David for Mephibosheth the son of Jonathan: "So Mephibosheth lived in Jerusalem, for he ate at the king's table regularly. *Now he was lame in both feet*" (2 Samuel 9:13, NASB, italics added).

Let's Talk to the Lord Together

3

Let's Talk to the Lord Together

> Who knows how much cancer, arthritis, and heart disease could be healed if only ordinary Christians learned how to pray with one another.[1]

When was the last time you shared a struggle with a Christian friend and heard the familiar response, "Hey, I'll pray for you"? You probably said, "Thanks" and walked away. Perhaps you should have asked, "When?"

I think I've heard thousands of people over the years tell me that they would pray for me. I am not doubting that they prayed for me or still continue to do so. But to me the distant, nonspecific "I'll pray for you" seems rather impersonal. There are many times when I wish the vague promise would have been moved into the urgent moment of *right now* rather than *sometime later*. We all have some prayer needs that are better served by being added to a long-term list. Others, though, tend to be the "right now" variety. That doesn't mean we need to have God respond right now. It simply means that we sense an urgency to make the need known to God through others immediately.

I have come away from speaking at many conferences and seminars over the years tired and worn out in spirit. I feel fulfilled and totally drained at the same time. I have prayed for others publicly and privately at many of these conferences. Yet in all those miles of traveling and speaking, only three times has an audience prayed specifically for me and what I was about, or about to be about in the days ahead. And believe me, when prayer like that happens, it is a wonderful thing! Praying for one another provokes a sense of care and concern mingled with love that seems to sweep over you and refresh you. There is also a bonding that takes place between you and those praying specifically for you. These prayer times are so special that I wonder why more people don't do it. Then I wonder why I don't do it more. And the doing or not doing is what we want to talk about in this chapter.

Prayer Is Not Optional

Perhaps the strongest admonition in this area is found in James 5:16: "Therefore confess your sins to one another, *and pray for one another*, so that you may be healed. The effective prayer of a righteous man can accomplish much" (NASB, italics added).

This verse seems aimed at life in the Christian community. The "one another" is definitely a community concept. It reveals that there are some things we need to do with our brothers and sisters in God's family. Confession is one thing and prayer is another. The thought of doing either with our closest circle of Christian friends can be scary. Confession, if not followed by prayer, can become instant gossip. Prayer in this instance should seal the confession before God.

Praying for one another is instructed and practiced throughout Scripture. It was the bond of love that drew people together in Christian community. When the difficulties of life and the opposition of Satan bore down upon the early Christians, they met to pray together. Hope was revived when Christians prayed together. With New Testament Christians, corporate prayer was a "given" rather than an option. But with twentieth century Christians, it seems to be barely an option any longer.

The weekly church prayer meeting, where individual and collective needs were shared and prayed for, has been deleted from many church calendars. It has been replaced with film series, seminars, classes, family nights, potlucks, and other assorted items (all good and necessary in the proper place).

Prayer meeting was cancelled or replaced in many churches due to declining attendance and interest. In an age of sparkling, attendance-drawing programs, prayer meetings just don't seem to have the fizz. Perhaps it's because prayer is hard work. And how many Christians want to attend church to work?

Prayer times have been slipped into the local church calendar week almost like fillers. We pray for one minute here and four minutes there. The pastor prays the pastoral prayer on Sunday, and somebody offers opening and closing prayers for everything from softball games to car washes to choir concerts. Somehow we feel that if we pray at the beginning and end of something, God is bound to bless whatever falls in between.

Periodically, the church calls people to a day of prayer or a prayer conference when special needs arise. These events typically do not draw standing-room-only crowds. Most are sparsely attended. The once-popular early morning prayer breakfast has been replaced in many churches by a motivational speaker or Christian businessman who sends us charging into our day—in between an opening and closing prayer!

Some Prayer Hurdles to Overcome

I have noticed two other things concerning prayer in the churches around me. The first is that very few churches are open during nonservice times so that people can stop in for a few moments to pray. I would venture to say that only a few churches in my community are available for drop-in prayer. (Most of them are locked to keep the vandals out!) Even the few that are open are seldom quiet enough for prayer and meditation. Part of the problem is that we go to church today for meetings and more meetings. We are not encouraged to stop by for a few moments with God during our day. Yes, I know I can pray in the cafeteria at work or under the elm tree near the office. But being in the place of corporate worship can sometimes prompt us to individual worship and prayer when other locations turn our attention to unfinished tasks.

The second thing I have noticed is that very few people pray with one another informally when they're at church. When was the last time you saw little groups of people huddled together in prayer on the church patio, in the parking lot, in the corners of the church gym, or in the Christian Ed building? I am amazed how quickly we seem to shift gears after the benediction. It's as if everyone breathes a sigh of relief that we can now talk about things like brunch and football and other important things. Our Christianity is switched on while we're in the service but switched off at the final "Amen."

Even the church that has "Enter to Worship, Depart to Serve" inscribed upon its bulletin seems to struggle with flipping the serving switch on when the worship ends. Praying with others who have needs is service of the highest form.

How do we learn to bring prayer back into a place of importance in our lives? Swedish scholar O. Hallesby says in his classic book, *Prayer*, "Prayer is the most important work in the kingdom of God."[2] Apparently not many Christians today agree wholeheartedly enough with his statement to give prayer its rightful place of prominence in both corporate and individual endeavors. I want to share some of my struggles and suggest some answers that will free us in the area of prayer.

Will You Pray for Me?

Why is it so difficult for most of us to ask others to pray for us? I have several struggles in this area. First, I really don't want to bother anyone else with my personal problems. I know that other Christians have greater needs and burdens than I do, and I guess I don't want my problems labeled insignificant or relegated to place number 98 on someone's prayer list. Plus I don't want people to start giving me answers when I give them a prayer request. I want them to *pray*, not *preach*!

My second struggle is with my own pride. I want to believe that I am strong enough spiritually to wrestle through my concerns with God alone. After all, I am in the ministry and I should know how to do that. I have read numerous books on prayer over the years and have been in hundreds of prayer meetings. I should have an inside track on prayer if there is one.

Third, I am afraid of what the answer might be and afraid that those praying for me will also find out God's answer for me. You see, I still struggle with wanting things to work out my way rather than God's way. I don't want anyone else to know that I did not get the answer I wanted in prayer.

A fourth struggle is in the area of belief. Don't get me wrong; I believe in the power and importance of prayer. Belief here means, "Can I put God to the test, put Him on the line in front of my praying friends?" If they pray for something in my life that fails to happen, will they be embarrassed? Will I be embarrassed? Will I blame them? Calling on God privately keeps others from knowing the results.

I also have a tendency to ask people only to pray for small things so that the answer either way won't be a very big deal. It is safer to believe God for little things than for big things. It is safer not to pray specifically because then you can accept nonspecific answers. My lack of belief also says, "Would this have happened even if you had not prayed?" I know a little of the feeling expressed by the father who brought his son to Jesus for healing and said, "I do believe; help me overcome my unbelief!" (Mark 9:24, NIV).

A final difficulty for me centers on the mechanics and logistics of having others pray for me. Do I ask people for prayer only at church after the worship service? Can I request prayer in the living room or kitchen? Should we kneel or stand? Should we lay hands on each other? Should our prayers be brief or long? Can we pray just anywhere with people milling around? These questions tend to cross my mind especially when I am praying with friends rather than strangers. Maybe my defenses fall when I am with my friends and I feel too vulnerable.

Hanging in There in Prayer

Most of the needs we ask others to pray for don't have quick, easy answers. Physical ailments and emotional pains that we pray about often are resolved over an extended period of time. And human needs addressed in prayer (new job, larger home, etc.) are seldom filled with the snap of a prayer finger.

There is a great need today in the Christian community for long-haul caring through prayer. We need to be committed to remain persistent in prayer with one another until the answer comes from God.

I have asked for and received prayer in the past from people who have never checked back with me for a progress report on God's response to their prayers. I guess they moved on to bigger and more important requests. I am amazed when someone remembers to ask me about a prayer request I gave them many months before. It does happen, but not very often.

When Paul wrote to the early church at Thessalonica, he stated, "Pray continually" and "Brothers, pray for us" (1 Thessalonians 5:17,25, NIV). Both of these phrases have a ring of persistence about them. The asking, seeking, and knocking that Jesus talks about in Matthew's gospel implies persistence (see Matthew 7:7,8). I believe that same persistence needs to prevail when we commit our prayer needs to our friends. It is no sign of weakness of faith when we can say to those who have prayed for us in the past, "Continue to pray for me."

The People Part of Prayer

I believe that there are three basic prayer arenas in our spiritual journey. The first arena is individual prayer. There are times in our day when we need to be alone with God in prayer. Scripture tells us to "Go into your inner room, and when you have shut your door, pray to your Father who is in secret, and your Father who sees in secret will repay you" (Matthew 6:6, NASB). Some translations use the word "closet" instead of "inner room." The real message is, "Get alone with God." Having special places for prayer is important. It can be a room in your own home, a special place in the middle of God's natural creation, or a quiet worship center. It can also be a retreat location you travel to on special occasions. Many of my friends go to monasteries for extended periods of uninterrupted prayer.

The second arena for prayer is one's immediate family. Francis MacNutt, in his book titled *The Prayer That Heals*, says, "This lack of shared family prayer is a terrible loss, and it's so common that married couples don't even realize they are missing anything. You seldom hear a sermon about praying together; yet, it seems to me, missing out on shared prayer is a loss similar to not attending church on Sunday."[3] He goes on to say, "So far as I know, there is no teaching in any Christian church against praying together at home; in fact, quite the contrary."[4] What MacNutt says, and what most of us know, is that the family arena for prayer is vastly neglected today. Perhaps the Catholic slogan of a few years ago has some merit: "The family that prays together, stays together." Praying as a family has diminished much like eating as a family. Distractions, busyness, jobs, personal agendas, and friends have all chipped away at family times for prayer. The only thing that seems to bring families together for earnest prayer from time to time is a crisis.

The third prayer arena is the circle of your closest Christian friends. For most of us, this is a small circle. It is comprised of those who know us best and who love us in spite of our shortcomings. They are people whose spiritual journey, growth and maturity are closest to our own. It is with these friends that we can be most open and vulnerable in prayer.

Some of us might add a fourth arena here in the form of a larger Christian community or church family. We can request the prayers from this larger body, but the prayer experience is less personal and you never know who was really praying for you and who was not.

All three—yes, even four—of these arenas for prayer are places where we need to be praying for one another. Prayer must start in the privacy of our own closets, but should spiral out from there to encircle those closest to us, those we must touch through effective intercession.

Catch the Prayer Moment with Others

As we move daily through the Christian community and the not-so-Christian community, we hear many personal needs and concerns expressed. When was the last time you responded to a spoken need by asking, "Would you like me to pray for you right now concerning that matter?" We may think an on-the-spot prayer may be appropriate, but we seldom verbalize it because of the uncertainty of the response. And we don't really want to invade someone's space without an invitation.

Most hurting people I encounter are just waiting for someone to offer to pray for them, even those who don't profess faith in Christ. Praying for someone is a positive, loving act that says we care and reflects God's care. Asking God to meet someone's need in prayer says that their needs are important to us. Even if no specific needs are expressed, a general prayer for God's blessing will send a person on their way aware of God's love in whatever lies ahead.

I am increasingly convinced that we should pray with and for each other at every opportunity. We need to think about catching the prayer moment with those whose paths cross ours each day. I have missed thousands of opportunities to pray for others because of my own insensitivity and hurried schedule.

I want to change that pattern as I know you do. Catch that prayer moment!

Because we are social creatures, we enjoy doing many things with our friends. Most of those things we do easily and spontaneously. But planning a time to pray with our friends does not usually come as easily or naturally. We can always think of something else to do before we think of praying together.

What would happen if you invited a few friends over specifically to pray—no dinner, no dessert, no small talk, just a time of prayer together? Would they think you were just being super-spiritual? Would they come anticipating an ominous and impending crisis in your life? Would anyone even come?

As we strive to develop warm and comfortable Christian friendships, we should also strive to develop a prayer relationship in those friendships.

In her book *Clinging*, author Emilie Griffin says, "Between Christians who pray there is a magnetic field; an attraction more powerful than any merely human passion, but like human passion. The passion of this friendship drives us to holiness. That is its distinguishing mark."[5]

Group prayer relationships must be encouraged to grow. Most of our prayer forms have come from our church life. They usually consist of singular speeches to God that have a beginning and an ending. We talk, God listens, and we go home. When we pray with our friends, we have the chance to move beyond formal prayer methods and employ many forms of corporate communication with God. Praise, confession, adoration, thanksgiving, intercession, petition, and worship are all viable ingredients of prayer. We must explore them and welcome them into our times of prayer with friends. Venturing into new prayer experiences makes us all nervous. But I am confident that the joy of growth will outweigh the tension of moving out of your comfort zone.

Spiritual Closeness Comes through Prayer

Paul was making a stopover in Miletus. While there, he sent for the elders from the church at Ephesus. When they arrived, Paul addressed them with one of the great farewell speeches of his ministry. After his address, Scripture tells us that "He knelt down and prayed with them all." Their response to that very warm and special occasion is recorded: "And they began to weep aloud and embraced Paul, and repeatedly kissed him" (Acts 20:36, 37, NASB).

This collective show of emotion occurred not because Paul was on his way to Jerusalem with the consequences of the trip hanging in the balance. Rather, these were people who had worked, planned, prayed, studied, laughed, and cried together in the past. Their corporate spiritual journey had drawn them together to share the human expression of what was to be their last meeting together on earth. When Paul could encourage and instruct them no more, he simply prayed for them.

One of the greatest ministries ordinary Christians have is that of prayer for one another. You will never be any closer to your Christian friends than when you are lovingly involved in vital prayer experiences with and for them.

The Gentle Art of Spiritual Friendships

4

The Gentle Art of Spiritual Friendships

Friendship comes to us in many forms. Most of us have a circle of friends that dates back into our history. The things we have shared over many years of intertwining our lives draw us close to one another. Friends are people with whom we share the celebrations and defeats of life. They are there for us in the good times as well as the bad times. To be a friend means to be a person for others.

New friends continue to come into our lives if we are willing to open the door to them. Some friendships seem to ebb and flow with the years. Some who were once close are now distant from us. We often wonder why. Have we changed so much? Have they changed? We search for new friends to replace those who have faded from view. In all of our struggles for friendships, one thing rings clear: We need all the friends we can get in our journey through life.

As I counsel with people from time to time, I often ask if they have one or two close friends with whom they can share their struggles. I am constantly amazed how many admit that they have no close friends. In order to survive in our journey through life, we need to have friends.

Dr. Stephen Johnson, speaking about our need for friends, asks these questions:

* Do you have at least one person nearby whom you can call on in times of personal distress?
* Do you have several people you can visit with little advance warning without apology?

* Do you have several people with whom you can share recreational activities?
* Do you have people who will lend you money if you need it, or those who will care for you in practical ways if the need arises?

This list can be used to evaluate the friends in your life right now. It also puts friendship requirements on a simple basis. As we think about friendship in this chapter, I want to move our thoughts from the basics of human friendship to principles of spiritual friendships.

You Need a Friend

In his book *Spirituality for Ministry*, the late Urban T. Holmes explores the concept of being a spiritual friend:

> To be a spiritual friend one must have detachment, discretion and discernment, with all that prepares for these gifts. Spiritual companionship is a gentle art, demanding a willingness to listen as if one had a third ear attuned to the inner self. It is neither psychotherapy nor is it the sacrament of reconciliation. Sometimes one needs to confront, but far more often the best intervention of the spiritual guide is, in parabolic language, nudging the friend into a new way of seeing. The journey belongs to the other and that person's uniqueness must always be honored.[1]

Holmes continues,

> What do people want in the person who becomes a friend of the soul? (spiritual friend) The answers include greater spiritual maturity, the obvious presence in them of the Spirit, a willingness to listen, a liberal amount of holiness, compassion, a total commitment

to the other person's needs, an inability to be shocked, compatibility, honesty, confidentiality, and kindness.[2]

In recent years I have come to believe that one of the greatest needs within the Christian community is the development of spiritual friendships. Too many of us try to live out our Christian faith behind the mask of a spiritual Lone Ranger. This spiritual isolationism may well explain the lack of spiritual maturity, accountability, and productivity in many Christians. The age-old idea that faith in God is a private matter may be the reason for our inability to build solid Christian community through a network of vital spiritual friendships.

In the gospels, Jesus set an early example for spiritual friendships when He instructed the disciples to go out and minister two by two (see Mark 6:7). Later, when the 70 were sent forth, the same instruction applied (see Luke 10:1). I believe Jesus was showing His disciples that faith and life were to be shared in close proximity to relationship. And Jesus called His disciples friends instead of servants after He had shared with them all the things He heard from His Father (see John 15:15).

Friendship with God and with one another always comes from a strong spiritual center. On the human plane, Jesus' disciples had little in common with each other beside their commitment to follow Christ. The friendship which ultimately formed between them grew from a spiritual base. And that friendship grew stronger over the remainder of their lives.

Foundations for Friendships

Christian friendships today seem to be based upon our church or denominational affiliation, our doctrine or belief system, and which Christian celebrities we like and don't like. Our reasons for forming spiritual friendships seldom line up with those of Tilden Edwards who, in his book *Spiritual*

Friend, says: "A few years ago I interviewed 29 spiritual leaders, most of them experienced directors, most of them Christian, concerning the most important qualifications for a spiritual companion. There was basic agreement around these qualities: Personal spiritual commitment, experience, knowledge and humility, and an active discipline of prayer/meditation. The capacity to be caring, sensitive, open, and flexible with another person, not projecting one's own needs or fostering long-term dependency."[3]

Most of us would count it a high privilege to have a spiritual friend with the above qualifications. We all need someone who is a little farther down the spiritual road than we are, tugging on our spiritual coatsleeves to bring us along. Too often we find ourselves being bulldozed, steamrolled, divebombed, and blitzed into spiritual growth by our well-meaning Christian friends. Seldom are we nudged, loved, and encouraged to spiritual growth in an atmosphere of understanding. Perhaps this is why we often find it easier to be with non-Christian friends than with those who share our pilgrimage. Yet our need persists to find those who can walk the Christian road with us and be our spiritual friends.

I believe the need for spiritual friends is greater today than ever before. Many are attaching themselves to spiritual gurus when their real need is for one or two spiritual friends. In order to have a spiritual friend, several things need to happen:

1. You must sense the need for this kind of friendship.
2. You must begin praying for the Lord to send the right person into your life. There are many dangers in just latching onto someone you think fills the bill without asking for God's wisdom in the matter.
3. You must be willing to ask for and receive direction.
4. You must be willing to be spiritually accountable to another person—not an easy role in a do-it-yourself era.
5. You must give the relationship time to form and grow.

Investing time in a spiritual friend is an ongoing commitment.

6. You must spend time with your spiritual friend. I'm not talking about time for small talk or socializing. I mean spiritual review time—time to talk about the inner things of your heart and spirit, time to pray and develop long-term plans of action for your continued spiritual growth.

What Is a "Spiritual" Friend?

I have talked with people who tell me they have many spiritual friends. What they mean is that they have many friends who are reasonably spiritual. When I ask what they talk about with spiritual friends, they respond by saying, "Everything," which loosely translated means, "Nothing very important." I believe most of us have a deep hunger to discuss spiritual matters with spiritual friends, yet we seldom do so because of fear, discomfort, or distrust. Many are reluctant even to talk with their pastors fearing they will be judged spiritually ignorant or be given a barrage of quick, surface-level answers to questions they might raise.

Spiritual friends talk about the things that Mary and Elizabeth must have talked about in the three months they shared together. We only find the initial conversation as it is recorded in Luke 1:39–56, but that dialog alone sets the stage for many deep, personal discussions between Mary and Elizabeth which must have followed. And I am sure they didn't just talk about pregnancy and raising children.

Alan Jones, in his excellent book, *Exploring Spiritual Direction: An Essay on Christian Friendship*, says:

> There are in the Eastern Church, four simple requirements for a spiritual guide (friend). The first is love: not any kind of love, but an openness and readi-

> ness to accept another into one's heart. It is a love that takes time and is open to the possible anguish involved. The second requirement is discernment. This requirement is the heart of spiritual direction. Suffice it to say here that discernment is a charism (a gift) of the Spirit. The third requirement is patience. This may seem obvious, but it is no easy thing to sit and wait. We are tempted to make quick judgments and are either too relaxed or too harsh in our dealings with others. The fourth requirement is utter frankness and honesty on both sides of the relationship. It requires a naked trust which will set the tone of a relationship and will enable both to go very deep, beyond mere reaction to the impulses, drives . . . and energies that stir us up. Finally the Eastern tradition demands that the spiritual director be willing to embrace solitude and cultivate detachment so that he or she may be more available to what God, the Holy Spirit is doing in the individual human heart. Spiritual direction, therefore, requires a great deal of sensitivity to others.[4]

Spiritual friends desire the opportunity to give spiritual direction to those whom the Lord has drawn around them in a Christian support system. The tremendous responsibility to provide spiritual guidance should not be taken lightly. Those who receive help and direction from you will eventually share what they have received with others.

Preparing for Spiritual Friendship

In *Spirituality for Ministry*, Urban Holmes shares four guidelines for spiritual companionship:

1. The reading of Scripture and Christian spiritual classics.
2. A time for solitude and silence (i.e., being alone with

God in a posture of listening).

3. Vocal prayer (a good test of our vision is the nature of our intercessions and petitions).
4. A provision for an ongoing plan of action.[5]

Holmes goes on to state, "We have to be rooted in what feeds our soul . . . the intimate knowledge of God . . . that the sweet meat within may grow and be there to feed the hungry."[6]

We do not generally talk about spiritual matters to others with freedom. If we converse at this level at all, we do so cautiously lest we be misunderstood or deemed to be superspiritual. I have spent time with many groups of ministers across America and have noticed how easily they talked about church work with one another but how seldom they talked about matters of the heart and spirit. If such hesitancy exists among those who lead, how widespread is it among those who follow?

Having a spiritual friend and being a spiritual friend means bringing God into the open space between our lives and allowing Him to do His work through each of us.

Out of the Grandstand and into the Game

5

Out of the Grandstand and into the Game

As a sports enthusiast, I have never been a good spectator. Even though I enjoy attending games, sitting in the stands with the crowds, and cheering for my favorite team, I confess to an inner itch to be on the field playing in the game with the contestants. I really don't want to collect my share of bumps and bruises, but I would like to know the thrill of receiving a 50-yard pass and racing into the end zone for the score. And what fun it would be to catch the puck on the end of my hockey stick and weave through the opposing team to score the winning goal.

Apparently the fantasies of my childhood and my active years in sports participation have never left me. I still pick up baseball gloves in sporting goods stores and try them on. I still want to buy a shirt with my favorite team's logo on it and wear it wherever I go.

For many of us, it is more fun to play the game than to sit on the sidelines and watch others play it. Yet most of us can identify with the description of the average sporting event: "Twenty-two men on the playing field are in desperate need of rest while fifty thousand fans in the stands are in desperate need of exercise." Some days, cheering just isn't enough.

Who Are the Players?

I have a growing feeling that many of us in the Christian family fall into the latter category of those in desperate need of exercise. Some of us sit in the church stands week after week watching the tired professionals in ministry who are desperately in need of rest. They keep trying to get us in the game and we keep trying to get them off our backs. And those of us in the church stands seldom encourage the playing staff. Jeering often replaces cheering. Criticism replaces caring and helping. Somewhere in the Christian journey we have thoroughly confused the roles and responsibilities of the players and spectators. We have forgotten the principle that *all* Christians are players. None of us belong in the stands; we all belong on the playing field.

Somewhere in the past, a band of tired Christian "players" went out and hired some "professionals" to do the work of the ministry. And the parade marches on. The Christians in the book of Acts were very involved activists in their walk with God and one another. But, sadly, many Christians today consider themselves only casual observers while the ministry is carried on by those who receive a paycheck for their labors.

I was in a church recently where the bulletin cover stated: "Ministers—the people; Pastor—John Brown." Was it true that the people in this church were really the players and that the pastor was merely the coach? If so, then this group of believers really understood that ordinary Christians were players and not spectators.

The Role of the Coach

Unfortunately, in some churches the professionals in ministry like to keep their people in the role of spectators. These church pros like to appear all-wise, all-skilled, and all-trained while subjugating the laity to subservient and menial roles in the life of the church. I have often wondered why bankers, engineers, and other professionals are given no more responsibility in some churches than ushering. I wonder why educators in daily life become spectators of religious education in church life where their expertise is seldom requested or appreciated.

I also wonder why many church leaders do not encourage their people to read, study, think, and grow. Perhaps it is because they do not want their own position challenged by the supposed casual observers of the faith. I believe that pastors should insist that their people read and study what they are reading and studying. I seldom see a pastor holding a book up on a Sunday morning and saying, "I want all of you to purchase this book today at our book table in the lobby and begin reading it this week. Talk about it to one another. It is exciting and challenging, and it will help you grow." Is there a fear among professionals that parishioners will be as well-informed about matters of the faith as they are? Some blame for lethargy among the players could be due to lack of challenge from the coaches.

I am not sure that a worship service is always the place for the pastor-coach to give his players a locker room pep talk. But I know that encouragement from leadership is as needed in the church as the coach's pep talk to their players before the game. "Win one for The Gipper!" could become "Win one for the Lord this week—and check back with me at halftime to let me know how it is going." As every coach walks the sidelines with his players, so the pastor and his staff walk the weekly sidelines with those of us involved in day by day ministry.

There is a challenging account in Luke 10 of a group of passive spectators of the faith who became excited players. Jesus sent a large group of followers in pairs on a short missionary journey to speak about and perform the deeds of Christ. Jesus challenged them to a "hands on" ministry with people. Luke 10:17 reports that "the seventy returned with joy, saying, 'Lord, even the demons are subject to us in Your name' " (NASB). For the 70, the ministry of Jesus became something they did, not just something they observed.

Let me offer one caution on the subject of thrusting people

into ministry. There is a danger that some Christians will charge haphazardly onto the field of church activity because they feel they should be doing something. But it is important that people are spiritually prepared for their active participation in Christian ministry. And the need for preparation is as true for the "practical" ministries of the church (ushering, serving on committees, decorating for a banquet, etc.) as it is for the "spiritual" ministries (teaching, preaching, witnessing, praying, etc.).

Such preparation includes seeking God's direction as to where and when to serve, submitting to training and preparation, praying for the inspiration and the energy of the Holy Spirit to accomplish the task to the glory of God, and following the direction of those in authority. Without prayerful preparation, the work of the church—true ministry in Jesus' name—can become mere church work—religious jobs done to keep an organization functioning.

Moving from Spectator to Player

The question that makes the rounds at most pastors' conferences is, "How do you get the laity of the church involved in the ministry of the church?" Hundreds of books have been written attempting to answer the question. New programs are being spawned and many seminars are being conducted to address this issue. We may all soon be buried on the playing field of our faith under an avalanche of printed programs.

Perhaps the real question we should ask about lay involvement is, "How did Jesus do this with His disciples?" The first thing that strikes me from Scripture is that Jesus prepared Himself for His ministry before He prepared anyone else. He spent time before His heavenly Father in solitude and prayer on a regular basis. He moved about with certainty and surety because of His personal preparedness.

I sometimes wonder if Jesus ever asked the Father, "How

would you like this task done?" How much better prepared to be a player would you and I be if we constantly asked God that question in the things we face. It is too easy to say, "I know how to do that," and then go and do it on our own strength and knowledge. We not only need to ask God the right questions, but we need to be willing to wait for His answer before we act. For me, and perhaps for you, the waiting is harder than the asking. I am never sure that I have as much time as God does.

Do As I Do

The second thing about Jesus' ministry with His disciples is that He modeled what He wanted them to do and become. In order to be a good model, He did not hide behind a desk piled high with books on theology and humanity. Rather, He invited His disciples, "Come follow Me and I will show you what I want you to do." They were present when He healed people, when He discussed issues with people, when He cast out demons, when He demonstrated His love, when He fed the hungry, when He calmed the angry seas. The disciples were witnesses to the power of His Deity as well as the frailty of His humanity.

It is easier today to be lost in a sea of committees than to be out in the sea of life with your committee. We desperately need leaders in ministry who are out there with the followers modeling the work of ministry. Many among us are not good players because no one is showing us how. We send our money to missions but few of us have been challenged to go watch missionaries minister. Pastors call on the sick, but how often are laymen invited to go along and learn the ministry of praying and caring? Church folk have become used to calling on pastors when a crisis invades their lives. We should also call on non-pastoral brothers and sisters and give them the opportunity to use their spiritual gifts in practical ministry.

Few people would debate the importance of the professional staff in ministry today. But the focus today must be on placing the ministry in the hands and hearts of the laity. The professionals are merely equippers and enablers. They are to be prepared examples and trainers of others for Christian service. An athletic coach may know all about the game, but his success lies in teaching what he knows to his players and getting them to play the game. You'll probably never see a coach run on the field, kick one of his players off the field, and take his place (even though I am sure some would like to!). There would be no world of sports if there were only coaches and spectators. Players make the game happen.

In his classic work, *The Incendiary Fellowship*, Elton Trueblood says:

> The glory of the coach is that of being the discoverer and the trainer of the powers of other men. But this is exactly what we mean when we use the Biblical terminology about the equipping ministry. A Christian society is made up of men and women whose powers in the ministry are largely unused because they are unsuspected. The Christian coach will be one who is more concerned, therefore, in developing others than in enhancing his own prestige. Ideally, he will not do anything himself, if another can be enabled to grow by being encouraged to do it.[1]

One of the current problems in the Christian community is that many pastors called to the role of equipper and coach have found out that they can receive more financial reward in ministry by becoming ministerial entrepreneurs. Many senior pastors are seldom found at home training and coaching. They tend to prefer traveling and "extending my ministry." I sometimes wonder if the kindest word God could say today to those called to be professionals on the church staff is, "Stay home and shepherd the flock." Modeling requires on-site attendance.

Power for the People

The third thing that Jesus taught His disciples about ministry was that they would receive power to be His witnesses all over the earth (see Acts 1:8). It is hard to be a participant in ministry if you are unsure of your source of strength. It is too easy to duck out the side door at the first challenge to be a minister to others. It is too easy to say, "I don't know how" or "I am not equipped for this."

In his confrontation with God at the burning bush, Moses tried to duck out on God's calling for his life. God's words to Moses were: "I will be with you" (Exodus 3:12, NIV). Those words are an encouragement to us today, assuring us that we will not be alone on the field of our ministry. God's power and promised presence are the equipment for our adventure.

Passivity and indifference are greater threats to the Christian than conflict, challenge, and struggle. Ordinary Christians will not settle for the comfortable seats of the grandstand. They will only be happy when they are down on the playing field of their faith experiencing the promises that Christ gave to those who would follow Him.

It is to those who are on the playing field that the words of Hebrews 12:1, 2 apply:

> Therefore, since we have so great a cloud of witnesses surrounding us, let us also lay aside every encumbrance, and the sin which so easily entangles us, and let us run with endurance the race that is set before us, fixing our eyes on Jesus, the author and perfecter of faith, who for the joy set before Him endured the cross, despising the shame, and has sat down at the right hand of the throne of God (NASB).

James Fenhagen, in his excellent book, *More Than Wanderers*, sums up our call to full involvement with these words: "The Christian journey begins when, as forgiven and affirmed people, we ever so tentatively risk letting our lives be shaped and empowered by the Person of Jesus Christ. As the Gospel proclaims, because He lives, we live also with new possibility and purpose. Instead of being 'takers,' we become 'givers,' members of a community struggling to live in a new way."[2]

Tuning in with Your Heart

6

Tuning in with Your Heart

Developing spiritual sensitivity is the process of fine-tuning our hearts to the heart of God. That's not an easy thing to do at a time when human insensitivity abounds and we are constantly told that only the tough and resilient among us will survive. On the human level, sensitivity is often looked upon as a sign of weakness. Sensitivity involves feelings, emotions, vulnerability, and needs. Since there is no safe, universally accepted method for the expression of these qualities, we keep them under a protective lid.

It is difficult, if not impossible, to develop spiritual sensitivity in our relationship to God if we cannot first cultivate sensitivity toward ourselves and those around us. Yet we tend to resist interpersonal sensitivity because of the possible pain involved. According to the dictionary, sensitivity is the power to perceive or feel. Deep feelings for someone can lead to personal involvement, and close personal involvement inevitably includes criticism. Often it is the fear of criticism that sends us running from close relationships to the hiding place of insensitivity.

Recently, the Los Angeles City Council voted unanimously to allow the homeless to sleep in the council chambers for three nights due to excessive cold temperatures. The council acted out of their human sensitivity to others' basic needs and they were roundly praised by some and condemned by others for their decision. Being sensitive usually puts one in the place of highest vulnerability. It is always safer to form a committee and study a problem for ten months than to take quick action to meet a pressing human need. By the time the study is released, the need is either gone or no one really cares about it any longer.

If you and I struggle to develop human sensitivity, how much greater is the battle to grow and strengthen our spiritual sensitivity? And is spiritual sensitivity really important in forming our walk with God? Will developing our spiritual sensitivity only alienate us from those in our Christian community who are less sensitive?

The Master's Touch

One of the greatest examples of spiritual sensitivity is found in Matthew 19:13–15: "Then little children were brought to Jesus for Him to place His hands on them and pray for them. But the disciples rebuked those who brought them. Jesus said, 'Let the little children come to me, and do not hinder them, for the kingdom of heaven belongs to such as these.' When he had placed his hands on them, he went on from there" (NIV).

The response of the disciples to this intrusion into Jesus' schedule would probably be much like our response to people we don't deem very important. The disciples felt that Jesus was only concerned about activities like healing people and teaching them. Children then as now were often looked upon as interruptions or nuisances and pushed into the background. Their needs can be put on hold until a more convenient time. But the parents who brought their children to Jesus really wanted only two simple things from Him—prayer and the placing of His hands upon them. Their request would take little time and attract little attention.

The ever protective (and somewhat jealous) disciples did not welcome the intrusion in any way. By sweeping the children aside, they were saying that Jesus had more important things on His agenda. I can imagine Jesus looking up as the children were pushed away and saying, "No, no. I *do* have time for them. They are just as important as anything else that I am doing today."

Jesus exemplified sensitivity in this encounter in several ways. First, He was sensitive to the parents and their reasons for bringing the children to Him. Their small request was not small in His eyes. Their concern was more than just to brag to their friends that their children had been touched by Jesus personally. The results of Jesus' prayer and touch in the lives of the children is not known. But the knowledge that Jesus had time for them must have caused the children to realize their importance in His kingdom.

Perhaps Jesus' greatest sensitivity to the children is seen in the fact that He took special time for them. One of the greatest gifts we can give to anyone is the gift of our time. We guard it, we value it, we possess it, and we also waste it. We never seem to have enough of it, and when we share it with others, we are affirming their importance to us at a deep level.

Jesus was also sensitive to the insensitivity of His own disciples. He was aware of their responses, attitudes, and actions toward those they ministered to. He called them to account for their insensitivity by rebuking them. Perhaps we need to respond similarly when we see insensitivity expressed around us.

Jesus also made the disciples aware of what we could call "divine interruptions." As I write today, my phone keeps interrupting my thinking and writing. I could easily switch on the answering machine and merrily type away. But even this early in the day I have received some urgent calls. For me, switching on the machine would be an insensitive response to these needy callers. We all live with various kinds of interruptions to our daily schedules. Being sensitive in this area often means allowing the divine to interrupt the mundane or even the important.

Along with making an important statement to His disciples, Jesus said something equally important to the throngs of people around Him that day. In caring for the children, He communicated clearly, "Everyone here is equally important to Me." No one was left out. He, in effect, proclaimed the entire message of the gospel by His simple act of sensitivity.

It is so easy to decide who is and who is not important in our daily trek through life. We tend to divide the people around us into two categories—the important and the irrelevant. Important people get our time while irrelevant people get swept into the corners of our life. Not so with Jesus. He touched all people with the same gentleness and care.

God Has Something to Say

The primary area for developing spiritual sensitivity is in our relationship to God. For me, the key to growing in this area is my ability to listen to God. Many of us have not learned to listen to God with the ears of our heart. To me, listening to God with the heart means practicing biblical meditation, practicing prayer, and absorbing the Word of God into our very being. We must reserve time in our schedule to be alone with God, minus all the daily distractions that rob us of concentration and attentiveness to Him. Perhaps the admonition of Psalm 46:10—"Be still, and know that I am God" (NIV)—means that we can only really hear God when our hearts are quietly attentive to Him.

Being sensitive to God for me means asking the question, "What is God saying in my life right now?" We all have many thoughts and ideas swirling about in our conscious and unconscious mind. We suffer from scattered attention and blurred focus in our purpose and activities. This may be why so many of us reach for the television knob at the end of the day. Watching TV requires little mental effort from overloaded minds.

If I ask God what He is saying in my life, I must be willing to listen for His answer. Listening takes time and effort on my part. God may speak more to us about one or two areas of our lives than others. His order of importance may not be (and seldom is) the same as ours. He is in our lives and He is not silent if we will but listen. Sensitivity starts with listening and should be followed closely by our obedience.

God Is at Work

Being sensitive to God also means asking the question, "What is God doing in my life right now?" Focusing on this question brings us to a daily awareness of God at work within us. Sensitivity to God's activity helps us lay claim to the promise of Philippians 1:6: "Being confident of this, that he who began a good work in you will carry it on to completion until the day of Christ Jesus" (NIV).

Sensitivity to God's work in my life means being willing to watch for the hand of God moving through all the facets of my Christian journey. If I am aware of what God is doing, I can cooperate with trust and confidence allowing Him to do even more. I will not try to block His work out of fear or selfish desire. Instead I will learn to thank Him and celebrate His working in me. I will also be free to share God's goodness with my brothers and sisters who will be strengthened by hearing what God is doing in me.

I realize that envy can intrude into the sharing of God's work. We have all looked at great things God is doing in others and secretly wished He were doing those things in us. We need simply to trust God in this area and accept His will for us.

Knowing what God is doing in my life today can more readily equip me to serve Him tomorrow. The Israelites, in all their wanderings, were constantly reminded of who God was and what God had done in their lives. Their God-blessed history gave them great strength when their future looked bleak. God always finishes what He starts in you and me. Knowing what God is doing also gives me a yardstick with which to measure my own spiritual growth. If I respond to what He is doing, I will continue to grow. If I ignore His work, my spiritual life will suffer.

There's No Time Like the Present

A third question I must ask is, "What would God like to do in my life right now?" Maybe we need to tack onto that question the words "if I would just get out of His way." We get in God's way primarily because we have our own ideas and plans, and all we want God to do is bless what we have conjured up. We keep trying to second-guess God and figure out how to get Him to do things our way. I think I have fallen victim to this process about ten thousand times or more. It was the wise person who said, "God's work done in God's way and on God's timetable will always receive God's blessings."

Discovering what God would like to do in my life is a daily quest. There isn't one big answer; God's plan has daily implications. We simply need to set our prearranged ideas and plans aside and let God give us daily direction to what He would like to do in and through us.

Tuning in on People

The second area for developing a deeper spiritual sensitivity is learning to be sensitive to others, especially in what we say and do to others. Our communication in word and action should always be tempered by the love of Christ rather than the expedience of the moment. Our prayer needs to be, "Lord, help me to be sensitive to where this person is coming from today in their own journey." Sensitivity often means listening to the message of the heart as closely as we listen to their words. Listening to the heart is a skill the Holy Spirit will help us develop.

We must somehow listen for the needs and hurts of others. We must try to hear the thoughts, feelings, and messages they are unable to put into words. We, in effect, must listen to people with the same attentiveness that we listen to God. Since most of us succumb to the pattern of "talk now, listen later," we will need to pray earnestly for God to equip us to listen first in order to be really sensitive to others. Good counsel usually comes from good listeners who have, in turn, been listening to the Lord.

Some days I wonder if anyone listens to God anymore. I know many Christians who preface everything they say with the words, "God told me. . . ." To many of those I want to reply, "You don't say. I wonder why He didn't tell me." If you are ever tempted to tell someone "God told me," make sure you heard it right. God gets blamed for a lot of things He didn't say!

Here are a few keys to developing spiritual sensitivity:

1. Be available to listen to God and listen to others.
2. Be fully attentive when you are trying to be spiritually sensitive to others. There is nothing worse than trying to communicate with someone who is tuned out.
3. Be willing to listen until you have heard everything that needs to be expressed.
4. Commit yourself to active caring through personal involvement and prayer support.
5. As you develop spiritual sensitivity to others, ask God what He is trying to say to you in each relationship. I believe God will speak to us when we approach relationships with an attitude of spiritual sensitivity.

Perhaps an entire book could be written covering the hundreds of areas of spiritual sensitivity. We have only hit the tip of the iceberg in order to place the need in front of you and help you be more aware of it in your own life. I don't want to go through life with my insensitivities increasing and my sensitivities decreasing. I want to develop the same awareness that Jesus modeled with the little children who came for affirmation in the midst of another busy day in Galilee.

You Are Responsible for Your Own Spiritual Growth

7

You Are Responsible for Your Own Spiritual Growth

We live in an era of spoon-fed Christians. There are more opportunities today for Christians to feast at the never-ending smorgasbord of growth opportunities than ever before. It would be impossible for any of us to attend all the conferences, retreats, banquets, symposiums, seminars, lectures, cruises, Holy Land trips, and Bible studies that dot the Christian landscape. We need an "Annual Guide to National Christian Events" in order to sort out what we should attend, consider attending, or not attend. Most of these prime events are advertised as the greatest ever with the most extensive line-up of Christian specialists ever assembled under one roof. Tickets are not cheap, but we can always save 20 percent by registering right now!

We can hardly escape the promotional bombardment advertising these varied educational and inspirational opportunities. Each one seems to be billed as the ultimate event, leaving the promoters scratching their heads wondering how to hype the next ultimate event. As one person recently said, "All you need to succeed in Christian event business today is a healthy mailing list and a good mailing service." The goal for most of these events seems to be to sell all the tickets, make a lot of money doing it, and bless the socks off the saints in the process.

In case you're feeling a twinge of guilt for attending the last three "greatest ever in Christian history" events, let me say that I am not against all Christian events aimed at helping saints grow. What I do oppose is the tendency for many Chris-

Christian growth menu. When Christian groups meet, the topic of discussion is often who went to what last, how many were there, and how great a blessing it was. And we just can't wait for the next brochure to land in our mailbox. We find ourselves living from great event to great event with very little to stabilize our lives in between.

Growing Is Serious Business

Christians today find it increasingly difficult to sit down with their study Bibles, devotional guides, and Bible commentaries to spend an hour studying the Word of God when they can turn on the TV and let someone else do it for them. It is easier to attend an all-day seminar on witnessing than to share your faith with your neighbor. It is easier to listen to people talk about prayer than to pray. Slowly and subtly, we are turning the responsibility for our Christian growth over to those who will do it for us.

We sometimes do this best within the confines of our local church. We pay the pastor and staff to teach us, and we nod our heads in approval and go forth after the benediction proclaiming the greatness of the message. We do little, if anything, to prepare for the Sunday message and we do less after hearing it. I often wonder how many would attend Sunday education classes or worship services if we were required to bring completed homework assignments. What if we were not allowed to even stay unless we had a textbook (Bible) and took notes during the teaching? I have yet to hear a pastor ask his congregation, "Did you complete your homework for 'Growing in the Lord' this week?" Nor have I heard a pastor say, "Take out a pencil and a piece of paper. I am going to give you a test on what you learned in your personal Bible study this week." Church overcrowding would seldom be a problem if that kind of challenge were issued each week. Or would more people come to church because personal Christian growth was so highly regarded?

I am always amazed that the requirements for maintaining membership in a community service club are far more stringent than for maintaining membership in the church. When I joined the Optimist Club years ago, I was required to contribute so many hours of community service each month. Also, if I missed any regular weekly meeting of the group, I had to attend another group's meeting in town to make up for my absence. And I complied very carefully with these requirements for the next four years until I moved to another city.

When I suggest to pastors that churches need to be more strict with growth requirements, disapproval is the general response. "We will lose members if we're more strict," say some. "You cannot legislate personal growth," say others. Still others argue that the church is to accept people where they are (and perhaps leave them that way).

I find that attitude standing in marked contrast to what Jesus said in Matthew 16:24, 25: "Then Jesus said to His disciples, 'If any one wishes to come after Me, let him deny himself, and take up his cross, and follow Me. For whoever wishes to save his life shall lose it; but whoever loses his life for My sake shall find it" (NASB).

If we asked every person entering our local churches on Sunday if they intended to follow Jesus, perhaps 99 percent would answer, "Yes." Maybe the next question we should ask is "How closely do you intend to follow Him?"

Jesus required self-denial, cross-bearing and following. Denial speaks of self-deprivation. Cross-bearing speaks of personal identification and responsibility. Following speaks of going in the right direction. I believe Jesus gave these stringent requirements to separate the serious from the curious. There is nothing wrong with coming to Jesus filled with curiosity and wonder, hoping to discover who He is and what He would do in our lives. But having discovered Him, there *is* something wrong with remaining on the sidelines of Christian growth instead of getting serious about the self-denial, cross-bearing, and following of Christian discipleship.

The Word on Spiritual Growth

One of the strongest Scriptural references for the need to grow was given to the Ephesian Christians. Paul said, "We are no longer to be children, tossed here and there by waves, and carried about by every wind of doctrine, by the trickery of men, by craftiness in deceitful scheming; but speaking the truth in love, we are to grow up in all aspects into Him, who is the head, even Christ" (Ephesians 4:14,15). A serious follower of the Lord today should have these verses emblazoned on his or her heart. The false winds of doctrine blowing across the Christian community today are at gale force. Sincere and well-meaning Christians are being blown off course every day. It seems to me that we are buffeted by two forces today in our struggle to grow in Christ—apathy and false teaching. The apathetic sit, listen, and do little. Those absorbing false teaching spend their time fighting windmills. Both errors are impediments to genuine Christian growth.

Peter instructed: "Long for the pure milk of the word, that by it you may grow," and, "Grow in the grace and knowledge of our Lord and Savior Jesus Christ" (1 Peter 2:2; 2 Peter 3:18, NASB). Luke recorded a summation of Jesus' personal growth in his writing when he stated: "And Jesus kept increasing in wisdom and stature, and in favor with God and men" (Luke 2:52, NASB). If there was ever a checklist for our personal growth, it is found in the four facets of this verse. Mental, social, physical, and spiritual development are all tied together under the need for growth. In this chapter we are emphasizing the spiritual aspect, but the other three are also important.

On the subject of growth in the early Christian community, Acts 12:24, reads: "The word of the Lord continued to grow and to be multiplied" (NASB). It does not say that the people grew and multiplied. God's Word must grow internally before spiritual growth happens externally.

Biblical standards for growth seldom line up with human standards. When someone says they attend a growing church, I want to ask, "What in the church is growing?" Much of the growth emphasis today is on increasing attendance and acquiring facilities. I wonder if such an emphasis is the result of following God's standards or the world's standards.

A recent ad in a religious magazine advertised a seminar titled, "How to Break the 200 Barrier." It stated in fine print that most churches in America have never exceeded 200 in attendance and that they plateau before they get to this stage. Since 80 percent of the churches in America today are under the 200 mark, the seminar should be well attended. My question here is: "Does numerical growth automatically lead to spiritual growth?" No, I am not opposed to churches growing numerically. I just wonder if our emphasis is correct.

Let's Get Personal

The growth emphasis in Scripture seems to be on the individual and his relationship with God. If spiritual growth and its emphasis is aimed at the individual, then the individual must assume the major responsibility for growing. If we are existing as spiritual infants, we cannot blame our pastor, Bible class teacher, or the Christian world in general. As a growing child learns to feed himself and assume responsibility for his personal hunger, so you and I must take personal responsibility for the major portion of our spiritual growth. We must learn the art of feeding ourselves spiritually, in spite of the fact that there are so many around us that we would rather blame for our immaturity. And even some of those voices would warn us that they are more mature and wise in the faith and can feed us better than we can feed ourselves.

Studying and memorizing Scripture is vital to our personal spiritual growth. But Bible study is more than stuffing our minds with verses and then spewing them out upon those who cross our path. The most important part of knowing Scripture is the application of its truth to our lives. We must continually ask about what we read: What does it mean? What does it mean to me? How can I make it meaningful to others? Knowing Scripture also sets God free to speak to me through what I know in a convincing and convicting way. The better I know God's Word, the more God is able to change me.

Along with biblical study, there are a number of other disciplines we can employ to encourage our own spiritual growth. Some of them are elaborated upon elsewhere in this book. But let me quickly share with you the homework agenda for spiritual growth.

Equal in importance to Bible study is prayer. Following these come silence, solitude, meditation, contemplation, Christian reading, the keeping of a daily journal (including notes and quotes), and Christian service. By Christian service I don't mean attending more meetings at your local church. Christian service means having one place *outside* your church where you "get down and dirty" in serving God. Serving at the local rescue mission, feeding the homeless, rebuilding an orphanage, etc., are great projects. Reading the local newspaper will give you enough project ideas to last a lifetime.

All of these disciplines combined encourage spiritual growth. They are not hoops to be jumped through. They are disciplines to be observed on a daily and weekly basis. They are exercises that build spiritual muscles and keep us strong and fit in the Lord's service.

Dedicated to Spiritual Discipline

8

Dedicated to Spiritual Discipline

> We must rediscover for ourselves the significance and the necessity of the spiritual disciplines. Without them, we shall continue to be impotent witnesses for Christ. Without them, Christ will be impotent in his efforts to use us to save our society from disintegration and death.[1]

One of the greatest pitfalls for the ordinary Christian today is spiritual dryness and boredom. Even though we live in an age offering a cornucopia of Christian events and resources to help us grow spiritually, we run the risk of withering away on the inside. We tend to rely on the external experiences to build and strengthen our inner spiritual life, only to discover that we do not grow strong spiritually just by reading books, listening to tapes, and attending seminars.The words of Romans 12:2 zero in on us with convicting clarity: "Don't let the world around you squeeze you into its mold, but let God remold your minds from within, so that you may prove in practice that the plan of God for you is good, meets all His demands, and moves toward the goal of true maturity" (Phillips). We are called as Christians to an inner spiritual journey where God, and God alone, does the heart work in us. The inner journey demands a quiet, disciplined walk with God. This journey is a lifetime commitment, not a temporary spiritual fad. And a perpetual inner journey requires a lifetime supply of inner spiritual resources.

Too few of us were told that a long road to Christian growth awaited us when we received Christ into our lives. Too often, salvation is seen as the culmination of a journey rather than the starting point. In many churches today, evangelism is emphasized and personal Christian growth is minimized. We are often told simply to attend all the functions of the church, read our Bibles and pray every day and we will be just fine. After a time, there is a danger that these basics will become so automatic that they will lose their meaning and substance in our lives, becoming mere religious exercises that assure one of acceptability in Christian community. Many Christians choose to live on this superficial level rather than embark upon an inner journey with the Lord. As a result of this one-dimensional Christian living, we become sterile Christians and impotent witnesses for Christ.

A Spiritual Hunger Awakens

I believe that Christians in general are finally beginning to realize the need for a deep, personal, spiritual walk with God today. I see evidences of this awakening in my travels across this country. There is a spiritual hunger growing in Christians' lives that can only be filled through a focus on the inner life in God. Surface activities and involvements cannot satisfy the inner man. There needs to be substance, content, and reality to our spiritual journey or we will wither and die along the Christian roadside. Spiritual disciplines which have been lost to the Christian community for centuries are beginning to reappear with a vitality closely akin to a revival movement.

Christians are beginning to realize that they cannot *give* what they do not *live*. Albert Edward Day says, "The power of a life, where Christ is exalted, would arrest and subdue those who are bored to tears by our thin version of Christianity and wholly uninterested in mere churchmanship."[2] If others are bored by the lack of what you and I are, it is certain that we will be bored ourselves. And that boredom will eventually render us ineffective for God in our personal lives.

We desperately need to reclaim the basics of Christian discipline to bring spiritual order to our lives and enable us to walk in the Spirit. Susan Muto, director of the Institute for Formative Spirituality at Duquesne University in Pittsburgh, says, "Continually discover God at the center of your being so that you can carry Him into the midst of your doing."[3] Richard Foster says, "Superficiality is the curse of our age. The doctrine of instant satisfaction is a primary spiritual problem. The desperate need today is not for a greater number of intelligent people, or gifted people, but for deep people."[4] Scripture repeatedly confirms our deep need for God. David said, "As the deer pants for the water brooks, so pants my soul for You, O God. My soul thirsts for God, for the living God" (Psalm 41:1,2, NKJV).

In a world that tears away at the very fabric of our lives, we are called to build an inner defense system to fortify us against the world, the flesh, and the devil. As ordinary Christians, we are called to renew the spiritual disciplines of prayer, silence, solitude, meditation, fasting, contemplation, retreat, study, and service. Because there are many good books available on each of these topics (see the bibliography), we shall only share a few thoughts in this chapter about each discipline.

Prayer

In chapter 3 we stated that ordinary Christians pray for each other—up close and right now. Here we want to share some thoughts about prayer as a journey and a discipline. I think of the disciples who, like us, summarized all of their thoughts on prayer in the words, "Lord, teach us to pray" (Luke 11:1, NIV). In giving the Lord's Prayer as a framework for prayer, Jesus was not saying, "And that's all there is to it!" He merely gave to the disciples an outline or basic pattern for prayer. Their journey was to begin from the pattern and move forward in prayer. From this beginning, the disciples moved ahead in the school of prayer. It is obvious that they grew in prayer from the results we see in their lives, first in the gospels and then later in the formative stages of the early church. Results in prayer always come from a firm grounding in prayer. Too many of us today expect results without doing the homework.

In his classic work *Prayer*, O. Hallesby says, "To pray is nothing more involved than to let Jesus into our needs. To pray is to give Jesus permission to employ His powers in the alleviation of our distress. To pray is to let Jesus glorify His name in the midst of our needs. The results of prayer are, therefore, not dependent upon the powers of the one who prays. To pray is to let Jesus come into our hearts."[5] Prayer begins with an open heart and open spirit, and with a desire for instruction.

Methods and forms for prayer can be learned by reading good books on prayer. What seems a primary difficulty for most Christians is the when and where of prayer. Two guidelines can be helpful in this area. First, it is important that we have a *place* for prayer. The Scripture tells us to pray in our closet, meaning a private place which is free from all disturbances and distractions. We have specialized areas in our homes for washing the laundry, studying, eating, and storing our possessions. But do we have a specialized place for prayer? I am aware that we can pray anytime and anywhere. But it is good to have a special place for planned times of daily prayer. It would be exciting if every Christian home today had a special place for prayer. Your prayer place can be set up to accommodate kneeling or sitting. It can have a few Christian symbols or decorations marking it as a special place. Some homes I have visited have a small kneeling bench in the place of prayer.

It is also important to have a special time for prayer. Praying only when you feel like it means you will seldom pray. We Protestants pride ourselves in being free from religious rituals. We are not required to pray in specified forms, postures, or languages. But, sadly, we have thrown out the discipline with the ritual. Purposeful prayer requires severe discipline, including the discipline of time.

Reserved prayer times should occur when we are mentally fresh and alert, and when our minds are not already filled with other agenda items. Prayer time, to be meaningful, should be prime time, not left over fragments of our day. Jesus not only had special places to pray, He also had special times to pray. His busy schedule never took priority over His times for prayer.

The journey of prayer is one of growth and exploration. What new things about prayer have you learned in the past year, month, or week? What is God teaching you in prayer? What is God saying to you in prayer? Are you spending time listening to God in prayer? Are things happening in your life and the lives of those around you because of your growth in prayer? Have you studied for yourself what the Scriptures teach about prayer? Are you reading more and more about prayer but find yourself praying less and less? Do you pray only when you feel guilty for not praying?

The journey in prayer for the ordinary Christian can be summed up in Susan Muto's words, "Prayer is many things, yet it is one. It is the soaring of the human spirit to meet and be with the Spirit of God. It is heart calling to Heart, the alone with the Alone, the finite before the Infinite, the temporal at home with the Eternal. In prayer our human misery finds solace and strength in God's mercy."[6]

Prayer, to be effective and growing, must become a daily discipline. If it is anything less than that, it is merely a spiritual Band-Aid instead of a life-support system.

Silence

The psalmist says, "Be still, and know that I am God; I will be exalted among the nations, I will be exalted in the earth" (Psalm 46:10, NIV). If there is any mandate for the spiritual discipline of silence, it is centered here in David's words. We can only listen and learn, know and grow if we observe the stillness that silence brings. In his classic book *The*

Way of the Heart, Henri Nouwen says: "In the sayings of the Desert Fathers, we can distinguish three aspects of silence. All of them deepen and strengthen the central idea that silence is the mystery of the future world. First, silence makes us pilgrims. Secondly, silence guards the fire within. Thirdly, silence teaches us to speak."[7]

We live in a noisy Christian world today. We are inundated with a constant barrage of Christian communication, much of it good and needed at times. We tend to equate sound with accomplishment. Silence, on the other hand, seems like wasted space that should be filled with words. There is an uneasiness in church when the pastor asks the congregation to be still and silent before God for a time. We want to get on with the program, the service, the schedule. Silence, if anything, appears to be an interruption. Seldom do we leave church remarking about the wonderful time of silence in the service. We are unaccustomed to living with periods of silence. Perhaps that is why we do not get clearer directions from God in our lives: we are unwilling to be quiet enough to hear His answers.

The discipline of silence is best observed by simply being quiet before the Lord each day for a time and allowing Him to put His thoughts into our hearts and minds. Effective listening is always best done in silence. Because God often speaks to us in a "still small voice," we must be silent in order to hear what He is saying.

In *Pathways for Spiritual Living*, author Susan Muto says, "In silence the scattered pieces of my life fall into place and I see again where I am going. Silence puts me in touch not only with the human spirit in all its richness, but also with the Holy Spirit. It opens me to the dimension of transcendence. I experience rest and peace. Silence becomes a sanctuary in which faith, hope and love are restored. It readies me to listen to words that ring with eternal truth."[8]

Is it any wonder that we live in a constant state of turbulence and flux when we do not observe times of silence before

God in our lives? Silence—find time for it. Silence—listen to God through it.

Solitude

There is a ski resort in Utah by the name of Solitude. But I would venture to say that there is more noise in Solitude than solitude in Solitude. Solitude means aloneness, privacy, or isolation. Solitude doesn't sound like a lot of fun unless you need to sleep for a week. Many of us run from solitude, preferring to be with others.

Solitude is not a natural part of our Christian existence. Being by oneself means confronting oneself without the supportive scaffolding of friends, schedules, events, and assorted distractions. Henri Nouwen calls solitude "the furnace of transformation." Too few of us want to edge up close to that furnace for warmth. In *Making All Things New*, Nouwen says, "Without solitude, it is virtually impossible to live a spiritual life. Solitude begins with a time and place for God, and him alone. If we really believe not only that God exists but also that he is actively present in our lives . . . healing, teaching, and guiding . . . we need to set aside a time and space to give him our undivided attention."[9]

Reserving minutes, hours, and days of solitude to be alone with God is not an option for the Christian, it is a requirement. I admit that breaking away for periods of solitude is especially hard to do unless you live in the wide open spaces where the population is measured in hundreds instead of millions. Most of us need to find solitude where we live by learning to block out sights and sounds in order to be alone. Basil Pennington, writing in *A Place Apart*, says: "There are many places apart for each of us: those we create, those we find, those created for us. Each is a gift and has its gift in us. Seek and you shall find. Taste and see!"[10]

The critical thing about solitude is that we find the time

and the place for it. Renewing one's inner self is born in the times and places apart for solitude. We all cannot escape to the mountains, deserts, or beaches for our times of solitude. We must ask God to bring us those times in our daily sojourns through life. Jesus made times of solitude a high priority in His life. Matthew wrote, "After He had sent the multitudes away, He went up to the mountain by Himself to pray, and when it was evening, He was there alone" (Matthew 14:23, NASB).

There will be times when we need the refuge of the hills for our solitude and prayer much like Jesus did. Don't be afraid to run to the place of solitude in your life.

Meditation

If there is any area of spiritual discipline that makes Christians nervous today it is meditation. This sensitivity is largely due to the recent popularity of transcendental meditation and other forms of eastern, non-Christian mystical religion. When someone says "meditation" we think of bald-headed mystics in saffron robes chanting mantras in smoky temples. We resist the idea of meditation because we fail to realize two things. First, the Bible directs God's people to meditate. Second, just because other religious groups practice non-biblical forms of meditation is no reason for us to ignore the discipline.

The dictionary describes meditation as the turning or revolving of a subject in the mind. The first biblical reference to meditation is found in Genesis 24:63: "And Isaac went out to meditate in the field toward evening" (NASB). You might ask, "What was he meditating about?" The following verses describe the arrival of Rebekah, whom Isaac married. He may have been thinking and praying about finding a wife.

Meditation appears again when the reins of Israel's leadership pass from Moses to Joshua. In Joshua 1:8, it says, "This book of the law shall not depart from your mouth, but you shall meditate on it day and night, that you may observe to do according to all that is written in it. For then you will make your way prosperous, and then you will have good success" (NKJV). Young Joshua is commanded to turn God's words continually in his mind. He was told first to think about God's word, then to do it. The rewards of prosperity and success would follow.

The series of references to meditation is found in the Psalms. Psalm 1:2 says: "But his delight is in the law of the LORD, and in His law he meditates day and night" (NASB). This verse describes the man who is "blessed." His meditation in God's law results in blessing. The good things that come to the person David describes come as a result of what he spends his time thinking about. His thoughts are centered on God.

There is a continuous thread of references throughout the Psalms that both instruct and guide one in the discipline of meditation (see Psalm 63:6; 77:12; 143:5; 119:15,23,48,78,148). David prayed that his meditation would please God: "Let the words of my mouth and the meditation of my heart be acceptable in Thy sight, O LORD, my rock and my redeemer" (Psalm 19:14, NASB).

Paul wrote specific instructions to Timothy concerning the ministry. Then the apostle said, "Meditate on these things; give yourself entirely to them, that your progress may be evident to all" (1 Timothy 4:15, NKJV).

In the excellent book *Alone With God*, author Campbell McAlpine says: "Biblical meditation will revolutionize your life when it becomes a continual part of your devotion and a consistent feature in your life. As the words of men swirl around you, you will discover that your meditation transforms your own communication."[11] Susan Muto adds, "Times set aside for meditation or reflective reading invite us gradually to let go of all that preoccupies our clockwork minds so that we can relax in the presence of the Transcendent. It draws us out of mediocre Christianity toward intimacy with God."[12]

Christian meditation, simply defined, is tuning out all of the jumbled thoughts in our mind and allowing God to fill our minds with His thoughts. It is giving God the opportunity to impact our thought processes. It is clearing our mental agendas so God may fill us with Himself.

Fasting

The thought of going without food for an extended period of time is foreign to most of us. If there is any message coming to us about food in our culture today it's "eat, eat, eat, enjoy, enjoy, enjoy." Prime time television programs are peppered with food commercials prodding us to eat something between dinner and bedtime so as not to feel deprived. We live in a food-centered society.

Christians are no less subject to our culture's preoccupation with food than anyone else. In the Christian community, the three f's—fun, food, fellowship—seem to be a central feature of church events. We cannot have fun and fellowship without food. We cannot have visitors in our home for more than an hour without offering them something to eat.

With food occupying such a major role in our lives, why suggest that the denial of food for a time is a needed spiritual discipline for our time? In *Celebration of Discipline*, Richard Foster says, "Scripture has so much to say about fasting that we would do well to look once again at this ancient discipline. The list of biblical personages who fasted becomes a 'Who's Who' of Scripture: Moses the lawgiver, David the king, Elijah the prophet, Esther the queen, Daniel the seer, Anna the prophetess, Paul the apostle, Jesus Christ the incarnate Son. Many of the great Christians throughout church history fasted and witnessed to its value; among them were Martin Luther, John Calvin, John Knox, John Wesley, Jonathan Edwards, David Brainerd, Charles Finney, and Pastor Hsi of China."[13]

The Bible concordance lists more than 35 references for

fasting, including those who fasted and their reasons for doing so. In the Bible fasting means abstaining from food for a period of time for spiritual purposes. There is no promise that fasting will make you more spiritual or induce God to shower you with blessings. Fasting is an attempt on our part to get serious with God in a very specific way. When we fast we set aside one of our important physical needs (eating) in order to focus more clearly on our spiritual needs, allowing God to speak to us in new ways.

The secular advantages of fasting are touted in our society today. Fasting is employed to clean out the body's systems and refresh and invigorate the physical self. Since our bodies are God's temple, Christians can benefit from both the physical and the spiritual aspects of fasting.

Richard Foster states: "Fasting can bring breakthroughs in the spiritual realm that could never be had in any other way. It is a means of God's grace and blessing that should not be neglected any longer."[14] A good evidence of what Foster is saying can be found in Acts 13:2, 3: "As they ministered to the Lord and fasted, the Holy Spirit said, 'Now separate to Me Barnabas and Saul for the work to which I have called them.' Then, having fasted and prayed, and laid hands on them, they sent them away" (NKJV). In this instance, the Holy Spirit's direction for Saul, Barnabas, and the church was revealed through the disciplines of fasting and prayer.

Fasting and prayer are linked together elsewhere in Scripture as they need to be in our lives. Review the Scriptural teachings on fasting and read several of the good books available. Then begin to incorporate this discipline into your spiritual journey with God.

Contemplation

Of the nine spiritual disciplines we touch on in this chapter, perhaps the most difficult one to grasp firmly is contemplation.

Many people look upon contemplation as thoroughly mystical, reserved only for those who live in monasteries. Others link contemplation closely to meditation, while still others think contemplation means staring into space and wasting time. Perhaps the simplest definition comes from the great Trappist monk Thomas Merton: "Contemplation is the light of God playing directly upon the soul. In the strict sense of the word, contemplation is a supernatural love and knowledge of God, simple and obscure, infused by Him into the summit of the soul, giving it a direct and experimental contact with Him."[15]

According to the dictionary, contemplation means "to look at attentively, to consider thoughtfully, to ponder." In Philippians 4:8, Paul gave us a list of positive qualities which we are instructed to think about or ponder. Thinking in our world is often considered unproductive work. We want tasks performed that will produce measurable results. Perhaps our task-oriented society has led many of us into being "doing" Christians rather than "being" Christians. We can more easily measure the results of our deeds than our thoughts.

There are no verses of Scripture specifically instructing us to spend time in contemplation. Yet we are told to consider and think about many topics and truths in Scripture and the process of pondering God's Word is contemplation.

In describing a form of contemplation called active contemplation, Thomas Merton says, "Active contemplation then demands thought and action and acts of the will. Its function is to awaken and prepare the mind, to turn the heart toward God, to arouse a desire to know God better and to rest in Him. It introduces the soul to the joys of the spiritual life. It gives him a healthy taste for things of the supernatural order and weans him away from the satisfactions of the body and of merely natural knowledge. Above all, active contemplation prepares the way for love."[16]

Contemplation becomes a natural part of our spiritual discipline as we move deeper into our inner walk with God. It does not come by force or the practice of certain observances. It comes as God allows more of His light to be shed on our journey. In the words of one ancient mystic who was asked why he was always smiling, "It is because I look at Him and He looks at me and we are happy."

Retreat

How many times in the past year have you escaped the everyday grind to spend 24 to 48 hours alone with the Lord? I can hear your guilt over the miles as you answer, "None." I can also hear you saying that you just don't have time for that kind of luxury in your life. And I hear you confessing that you would not know how to use the time wisely even if you had it to spare.

We all take vacations and seldom question the need or expense for them. Vacation time comes automatically with most jobs and usually doesn't come soon enough each year for most of us. Too often, however, returning to work after vacation is the real vacation for those of us who have not learned to use well the time off we have.

One of the greatest instruments for spiritual discipline in our lives is the periodic, planned, personal retreat. The extended time afforded by a retreat allows ample opportunity for evaluating spiritual progress. Our greatest enemy in the discipline of retreating is the rush of our day-to-day lives. Yet if we are to keep our spiritual balance, we must find the time to be apart with the Lord.

Consider these words of Scripture if you need a legitimate tug in the right direction: "The apostles gathered around Jesus and reported to him all they had done and taught. Then, because so many people were coming and going that they did not even have a chance to eat, he said to them, 'Come with me by yourselves to a quiet place and get some rest' " (Mark 6:30, 31, NIV). Too busy even to eat! Sound familiar? This statement could well describe our Christian comings and goings today. We not only need to retreat occasionally from our secular surroundings but also from our church settings. Perhaps God's strongest call to us today is not to get involved in more Christian activities but to take time away from Christian busyness for personal communion with Him. Taking time for spiritual retreat allows the seeds of new life and growth to be planted in our spirits.

How often should you retreat? There are two key times to escape to your quiet retreat. The first is when the stresses and tensions of life begin to outweigh your graces. The second is when you plan for it well in advance and have it on your calendar. Each will have a different purpose. The first deals with survival, rest, renewal, and quiet conversation with God. The second is for growth, planning and receiving God's directions for the days ahead.

Where can you go? Find a restful setting, such as a cabin, a condo of a friend, a hotel or motel away from everything, or a Christian camp which may have facilities for individual guests. There are also monasteries in many areas with guest facilities available at very low cost.

What should you do? There are numerous books in Christian bookstores offering plans for guided spiritual retreats. For example the daily devotional guide, *A Guide to Prayer for Ministers and Other Servants*, provides numerous retreat models.

Gordon MacDonald, in his book *Restoring Your Spiritual Passion*, says there are three ingredients we all need in our spiritual lives: "Safe places, still times, and special friends."[17]

Jesus knew the value of taking time away from His busy schedule. He even sent the crowds away at times so that He could retreat to His Father. Spiritual retreats are not easy to plan because your schedule will conspire against you to prevent you from taking the time. Retreating will need to become a spiritual discipline or it will never happen.

Study

I need not say too much here about the discipline of study since we touched on it in a previous chapter. I do need to tell you that developing a program of ongoing study in your Christian life is a spiritual discipline. Susan Muto puts it this way:

> Formative reading challenges us to listen with docility to spiritual directives found in texts of lasting value. We temper the busy train of thoughts that rush through our working day in order to dwell with texts that arouse our longing for God. Such reading done in a slowed-down way on a regular basis reestablishes our commitment to Christ while helping us to let go of peripheral concerns.[18]

We are told in Scripture: "Study to show yourselves approved unto God, a workman that needs not to be ashamed, rightly dividing the word of truth" (2 Tim. 2:15, NKJV). We understand this verse to mean the study of Scripture, and certainly God's Word is the central focus of our study energy. However, God has used many men and women over the centuries to write helpful books about Christian life and growth. Too few of today's Christians have read the great spiritual classics of the past. These timeless volumes still speak to us today along with many excellent contemporary writers. Augment your study of the Bible by reading good Christian books.

Planned study and growth should be one of your spiritual disciplines. I can attest to the value of study in my own life as I have pursued it for my own spiritual survival. If you study the books suggested in the bibliography, you will be well on your way to some new levels of growth in your life.

Service

Observing the disciplines previously mentioned should enable us to be better servants of Christ. There are two forms of service that are vital to our own growth. The first is the service project, such as rebuilding a mission station on an Indian reservation or delivering a load of clothing to an orphanage in Mexico. Service projects are usually short term with a specific start and finish. The missions department in most churches provides project opportunities.

The second form of service is our personal, everyday ministry in the lives of others. Susan Muto states:

> Christian service attends to and cares for others in one's here and now situation. There is no split between who we are and what we do. We display outwardly the spiritual values we keep alive inwardly. Others sense in this caring presence an integration between what goes on in our hearts and what happens in the consulting office, hospital, law firm, union meeting, or whatever. It is not unusual to hear people say, "Your heart is really in your work, isn't it?"[19]

Service is basically an attitude which, like love, needs to be expressed. If service is the culmination of the other disciplines, we can probably gauge our success in the inner disciplines by measuring the service we outwardly express. Yet we tend to be more inclined in our church life to line up and let the church wait upon us. We hire trained pastors to meet our every need. And if they fail to serve us as we desire, we move them along and hire some others. We have misunderstood the role of the servant in Christian community. In truth, we are all called to be servants. Richard Foster writes: "Service that is duty motivated breathes death. Service that flows from our inward person is life and joy and peace. The risen Christ beckons us to the ministry of the towel."[20]

Serving is not always a joyous experience nor is it always received with gratitude. It is tiring and often thankless. It can be repetitious and boring. It can leave the giver drained and empty. But the reward of service comes from the obedience. St. Teresa of Avila said: "Obedience usually lessens the difficulty of things that seem impossible."[21]

A Record of My Journey

Keeping some kind of record of one's spiritual pilgrimage and growth is essential to knowing where we really are in our inner walk with God. There are numerous ways to record our growth and numerous books telling us how to do it. I prefer simply jotting the thoughts, struggles, and growth of my walk with God in a spiral notebook. Some days there is much to write; other days, little; some days, nothing. At the end of the year, it is easy for me to look back through my notebook and see where I have been and determine how far I have journeyed.

Henri Nouwen's little book *The Genesee Diary* gives one idea of how to write reflectively of one's personal journey. Basil Pennington's *Jubilee* will also give some insight.

Try your hand at recording your spiritual journey and let God guide your writing. You will be amazed at how the recording of your disciplinary struggles will enrich your Christian walk.

The Art of Community Living

9

The Art of Community Living

Community usually refers to a collection of people with a certain lifestyle who have chosen to live in a certain locale. The dictionary says community is "a sharing or participation, an identity or likeness." Communities give strength, support, and identity to their members.

For the Christian, community means all the above and more. Community for believers is formed through Christian friendships in churches and other church-related organizations and functions. The form and format of Christian community is centered in the community Jesus established with His disciples which continued through the birth of the early church in the beginning chapters of Acts.

Christian community is best described as a group of fellow strugglers who share a common faith in Jesus Christ and a common expression of faith with one another. Henri Nouwen describes it in this fashion:

> A Christian community is therefore a healing community, not because wounds are cured and pains are alleviated, but because wounds and pains become openings or occasions for a new vision. Mutual confession then becomes a mutual deepening of hope, and sharing weaknesses becomes a reminder to one and all of the coming strength.[1]

What Nouwen suggests is that community for the Christian brings about healing from the pains and wounds we all receive in our journey through life. He strongly suggests that we work toward openness and sharing with one another in order to receive strength.

And if Nouwen is correct, community is better formed through the expression of weakness than through the expression of strength. Focusing on weakness is certainly not a widely accepted practice in the secular world and most of the time it does not have broad acceptance in the Christian world. It seems that the resounding cry today is, "Be strong for Jesus," when in reality we are completely acceptable to Jesus in our weakness. And those around us seem to identify with us more readily at the point of our struggles than in the celebration of our many victories.

How can Christians successfully weave the fabric of community so that it is mutually beneficial to all members? There are some biblical principles for building Christian community that can help us become for one another what God wants us to be. Some principles are easier to accept than others. Some seem to be all but forgotten in today's churches where the secular theme of "looking out for number one" has replaced the biblical directive of caring for each other.

Comfort One Another

Most of us are not proficient "comforters" because comfort is not always easy to express verbally. When a friend contracts an incurable illness or someone close to us dies, we fumble for the right comforting words to say. We easily forget that sometimes the best comfort comes simply from someone being there. Words can seldom heal the hurts our friends feel; but physical presence always seems to help.

Paul's letter to the Christians at Corinth directly addresses the topic of comfort:

> Praise be to the God and Father of our Lord Jesus Christ, the Father of compassion and the God of all

> comfort, who comforts us in all our troubles, so that we can comfort those in any trouble with the comfort we ourselves have received from God. For just as the sufferings of Christ flow over into our lives, so also through Christ our comfort overflows (2 Corinthians 1:3–5, NIV).

Paul talks about the legitimacy of the ministry of comfort. He nowhere says that comfort is only to be expressed to those who are weak. He knows comfort is something we all need at times and that God is the primary source of our comfort. Too often we feel that we must be the beginning and end of comfort to a hurting person or we will be of no value whatever. Perhaps one of the best ways to comfort others is to draw them closer to God who is the real source of all comfort. As they receive comfort from God and other believers, hurting Christians learn firsthand how to share comfort with others when it is needed.

In his letter to the church at Thessalonica, Paul encourages the early Christians to "comfort one another with these words" (1 Thessalonians 4:18, NASB), referring to the ultimate comfort that Christ's return will bring to all struggling with the world's system. In 1 Thessalonians 5:11, Paul instructs believers to "comfort each other and edify one another, just as you also are doing" (NKJV).

In today's Christian communities, as in the early church, there are always people in need of comfort and, hopefully, always people who are willing to dispense it freely and lovingly. How many fellow believers stand around us each Sunday in church aisles, patios, parking lots with a desperate aching, needing to receive comfort from brothers and sisters in God's family? Comfort, like love, is something that always must be shared to be beneficial. Sometimes the hurting need to open up and communicate their need for comfort. That kind of transparency is not always easy. Pride keeps the door to sharing well locked. Humility usually opens it.

An arm around our shoulders or a hand that holds our hand can bring an ocean of comfort to us. A prayer or a word of encouragement from Scripture can bring peace to a troubled spirit. The silent question on many lips today is, "Does anyone really care that I'm hurting?" The comforters can answer, "Yes!"

Pray for One Another

We have talked about prayer in detail in a previous chapter. Let me simply add here that praying for one another builds strong community. At least two positive things happen to us when we are prayed for by others. First, God begins to act in our lives in a way He could not before others prayed. Prayer moves God to act. Second, loving care is communicated when I realize someone is praying for me. Both of these results of prayer serve to fortify Christian community.

Forgive One Another

There are two ways that we are hurt by others. One is by accident, the other is by design. Both hurt, the latter usually more deeply than the former. The struggle to live in the Christian community depends in part on our ability to handle our hurts, regardless of the cause. We cannot live in community without being hurt at times. The old adage, "Christians aren't perfect, just forgiven," is of little comfort when one of those imperfect Christians hurts you. It is also naive to believe that if those around you were just more spiritual, they would not hurt you.

Ordinary Christians are called to live in community, and that means we must deal with the hurts which result from community living. We cannot avoid hurts in life unless we live alone in the desert or refuse all contact with those in the Christian community. So when people hurt us, we can either collect and store the hurts we experience and hold them against our offending brothers and sisters, or we can forgive those who hurt us and release them from their offense. The biblical way, of course, is to forgive.

One day, Peter came to Jesus with a question which had apparently been bothering him for some time. He had obviously witnessed and experienced the hurts which the religious community was aiming at both Jesus and the disciples. Wanting to know how to respond, Peter asked, " 'Lord, how many times shall I forgive my brother when he sins against me? Up to seven times?' Jesus answered him, 'I tell you, not seven times, but seventy-seven times' " (Matthew 18:21,22, NIV). Peter really posed the question, "Is there an end to this forgiveness business?" Jesus said that there wasn't. Forgiveness must keep happening because life and offenses keep happening. Jesus continued the discussion by telling the parable of the unmerciful servant, focusing on the reciprocal nature of forgiveness (see Matthew 18:23–35). If we don't forgive, we cannot be forgiven.

Sometime ago I was reading a leaflet on forgiveness in which the author stated, "Forgiveness frees the forgiver . . . and the person who accepts forgiveness, to love and to grow. It heals the spirit and heals relationships." He alluded to the fact that nonforgiveness locks people forever into separate prisons where they can no longer grow.

To live with a healthy spirit in a healthy community, one must practice daily the principle of forgiveness. Fellow Christians can wound us so deeply that we can end up living our lives in resentment, anger, distrust and bitterness if we refuse to forgive. The freedom to ask for and grant forgiveness results in healthy relationships.

Fellowship with One Another

The word "fellowship" is used only sparingly in the New Testament, yet it is used widely in today's churches. We schedule fellowship activities and fellowship meals. We enjoy fellowship after church and, if one arrives early enough, before church. Fellowship to many means a lot of people squashed together in a small place for a long time. The higher the level of conversation, the greater the supposed fellowship. The better the food, the better the fellowship.

The dictionary states that fellowship means "sharers or partakers in adversity or prosperity." We know about sharing prosperity, but Christians today seem to resist the fellowship of sharing adversity. Who in their right mind wants bad fellowship?

Yet fellowship in the Scriptures often meant sharing suffering and persecution together as members of the community of Christians. The concept of fellowship was also closely tied to one's relationship with Christ and His sufferings. Fellowship seemed to mean identification more than fun and good times. It always meant belonging—but to what? In the Bible, fellowship meant belonging to the company of believers. And being associated with the fellowship of believers in the first century meant suffering persecution together—not exactly the concept of fellowship we embrace today.

Fellowship in the Scriptures not only meant sharing the struggles of persecution, but also sharing the same joys. Their suffering drove them together to a oneness that few churches today experience. They ate together, prayed together, witnessed together, and considered their possessions available to any who had need. Let us hope that persecution isn't the only means by which we can learn to fellowship today as the early church did.

Serve One Another

Have you ever wished you could afford a staff of hired servants? Having servants is one of the greatest symbols of wealth and power in society. If you had servants, you would no longer be concerned with the mundane chores of everyday life. You could fill your days with career advancement and leisure pursuits, leaving the laundry, dirty dishes, vacuuming, and dusting to your "staff."

Everybody likes to be served. We eat at a restaurant occasionally and enjoy the service of a chef, waiter, and dishwasher. We climb the corporate ladder acquiring assistants and support personnel who do the paper work while we concentrate on wooing clients and increasing profits. Perhaps the ultimate American fantasy is achieving enough wealth and power to do only what you want while servants attend to your every need and whim. Even at church, nobody wants to be on the clean-up committee all the time.

Jesus placed servanthood in perspective for His followers in Luke 22:24–26: "A dispute arose among them [the disciples] as to which of them was considered to be the greatest. Jesus said to them, 'The kings of the Gentiles lord it over them; and those who exercise authority over them call themselves Benefactors. But you are not to be like that. Instead, the greatest among you should be like the youngest, and the one who rules like the one who serves' " (NIV). Jesus said that contrary to the world's view, His followers were to accept the servant's role no matter how important they may be. In fact, Jesus taught and modeled that the leaders were to be the primary servants.

A Christian community, like any secular community, is comprised of both leaders and followers. But the Christian community differs from the secular community in that the leaders are to be the chief servants of the followers. As such all believers are continually serving each other with no one always stuck with the menial responsibilities.

I tend to think that many in the Christian community today think that they are there to allow God the privilege of waiting on them hand and foot and meeting all their needs. We are in danger of confusing the role of servant and the served in our relationship to the Lord as well as in our relationship to one another. Jesus is Lord and we serve Him. We are also called to serve our brothers and sisters in God's family. It is only as we come to understand the real meaning of servanthood that we will build strong community. We are not to seek others to serve us in our Christian journey. Rather we are to seek others whom we may serve.

Love One Another

"Love one another"—this directive appears about 12 times in Scripture. One of the strongest uses of the phrase is aimed at the community of the disciples. They were even told that their identity hinged on their love for one another. Needless to say, this love did not happen in the church just because it was commanded. Love happened as it was lived out in practical ways, for love is something you do.

The activity of love builds Christian community. People will always move toward a community that expresses unconditional love. In a contemporary world where the demonstration of biblical love is often absent, we believers stand in position to offer others the love of Christ.

There are hundreds of ways to say "I love you" through acts of caring and kindness done in Christ's name. Most of us know how to perform many of these loving deeds. But there is one way of communicating love that we seldom employ within Christian community: looking a brother or sister directly in the eye and saying, "I love you!" It hardly ever happens to me, even though I know that there are many around me who love me but simply don't verbalize it. I believe our love needs to be verbalized often—and boldly! Hearing someone say "I love you" is affirmation of the highest level for those we care deeply about.

It is often difficult to say "I love you" because we don't want to appear mushy, sentimental, overreactive, or foolish. We need to learn a few more lessons about Christian honesty and expression if we are to build Christian community in which "love one another" is more than a slogan. If you want a challenge for the rest of this week, look for opportunities to say "I love you" as often as possible to those in your Christian circle. (And don't say it if you don't mean it.) Some pastors I know would faint dead away on Sunday morning if someone looked them in the eye and meaningfully said, "I love you, pastor." And some parishioners would do the same if their pastor said it to them.

Love builds community and ordinary Christians practice community. Henri Nouwen is right when he said, "Through the discipline of community we discover a place for God in our life together."[2]

How to Survive in the Wilderness

10

How to Survive in the Wilderness

> Thus the desert of which I speak is a desert of the spirit; a place of silence, waiting, temptation. It is also a place of revelation, conversion, and transformation. A true revelation is a very disturbing event because it demands a response. It involves being "made over," being made new, being "born again." The desert, then, is a place of revelation and revolution. In the desert we wait, we weep, we learn to live.[1]

For most of us, topographical deserts are vast expanses of dry sameness we would rather quickly drive through than settle down in. In spite of their stark beauty, deserts are subject to temperature extremes and survival challenges which only the hardiest and most adventuresome can endure. We would rather appreciate these arid wastelands from a distance or the air-conditioned comfort of our cars.

In this chapter, we want to share some thoughts about the importance of the geographical desert in Bible times, what it lent to the life of Jesus and others after Him, and what these desert experiences can teach us today. We also want to look at the inner desert in our lives—the desert of the spirit—and how to endure the dry times in our spiritual lives.

Welcome to the Wilderness

The physical desert or wilderness plays a prominent part in both Old and New Testament history. Israel struggled with the wilderness experience for 40 years. Their desert became a training ground for what was to come in later years. Moses hid away in the desert tending sheep after his hasty exodus from the courts of Pharaoh. His own 40-year exile prepared him to lead Israel for the remainder of his life. In spite of the hardships in the wilderness, God promised Israel through Isaiah that the desert would rejoice, bloom, and that streams of water would run through the desert's barrenness.

On the eve of His public ministry, Jesus spent 40 days and nights in the desert where He came face-to-face with Satan's temptations. When Satan was finished with Jesus in the desert, Luke 4:14 tells us that "Jesus returned to Galilee in the power of the Spirit, and news about Him spread through the whole countryside" (NIV).

One of the strongest messages these events convey is that the desert is not a place to be avoided. Rather, desert experiences are to be welcomed as the training and testing ground of our faith. The desert is a place where we fight our battles, test our faith, and even argue with God. Yet we can emerge triumphantly from these tough times better equipped to live.

The physical desert, in its vast barrenness, has a way of stripping us of our human support systems and forcing us to confront the real issues in life. The layers of protective armor melt away. Distractions are limited. Diversions are minimized. We are equipped to go "one-on-one" with God in a new way.

Again, an insightful word from Susan Muto: "When we follow Jesus into the desert, we are likely to experience what could be called ego desperation. Basically this means acknowledging that our life is not nor ever will be completely under our control. In the desert the pillars of human power, pleasure and possession are smashed. One feels powerless, miles away from sources of immediate gratification, the owner of little or nothing of material value. One cannot barter one's way out of loneliness and silence. One can only wait until it passes on the wings of faith and hope."[2]

Jesus not only escaped to the desert Himself while training His disciples and ministering to people, but He often took His disciples there with Him. He introduced them to the solitary place of both rest and wrestling. Perhaps the desert is the only place where these contrasting encounters with the Living God can take place. It affords an undistracted solitude and emptiness that few other geographical locations can offer. Escape and struggle are always close associates in the desert experience.

We enter the desert place in one mental, emotional, and spiritual state and hopefully exit in a better one as Jesus did. Alan Jones states, "From the point of view of the believer, the purpose of emptiness and desolation is to prepare us for joy and ground us in hope. Unless joy and hope are the goal, the desert becomes a playground for masochists."[3] Too few of us enduring a desert experience can clearly read the sign, "Joy and hope just over the next sand dune." We see only desolation, dryness, and isolation. I am sure Jesus saw the same things in the desert of His temptation but His emergence portrayed the victory of joy and hope we can all anticipate.

As one of God's ordinary Christians today, I am called to desert experiences in my life from time to time. I too go there to rest and wrestle and emerge with new hope, joy, and insight. I cannot survive in the crushing milieu of today's world without frequent desert experiences. Can you?

Footprints in the Sand

Perhaps the best known "desert people" after Bible times was a group referred to as the Desert Fathers. Being raised in the evangelical Protestant tradition, I had little knowledge of this largely Catholic group until I discovered some of their writings in recent years. The Desert Fathers were a group of Christians who moved from the cities to the severe deserts, such as the brutal Sahara, to avoid martyrdom. St. Anthony, the patron of the Desert Fathers, spent 20 years alone in the desert. When he emerged, he brought the strength of his solitude with him and shared it with many who came to him for a word of counsel. Those who visited St. Anthony described him as gentle, caring, and balanced. He so radiated God's love from his desert experience that others were drawn to him for spiritual ministry.

Others followed St. Anthony's example. Some remained in solitary isolation while others gathered in monastic communities. Thomas Merton said of the early Desert Fathers: "They knew that they were helpless to do any good for others as long as they floundered about in the wreckage. But once they got a foothold on solid ground, things were different. Then they had not only the power but even the obligation to pull the whole world to safety after them."[4]

Contrary to popular belief, the Desert Fathers were not simply escapists from the struggles of life. They retreated in order to know God better and share Him as they could with those who would seek them out. They feared, as many of us do, drowning in the swirling sea of life. But they discovered a desert place of refuge, albeit cold, hot, and hostile at times.

We have much to learn from the isolation of the Desert Fathers that will help us live with balance in today's world. Their gentle wisdom that grew from daily reliance upon God for all their needs can teach us much about how to live simply today.

Your Desert Days

Enduring a spiritual desert experience finds many parallels from a life of isolation in the geographical desert. We are accompanied by many of the same feelings—aloneness, emptiness, dryness, barrenness, rejection, sterility. Susan Muto states: "Illness or failure, any form of personal deprivation, reminds us of our need for Him. These events are desert messengers, heralding the Transcendent. They tell us to pause a while, to turn to God in prayer, to reappraise our life direction."[5]

The dry times of our lives cause us to ask, "Where is

God?" And we often hear no response, as if we have been abandoned by God. Biblical accounts are rife with stories of people who felt forgotten by God. It was Job who said, "God's terrors are marshaled against me" (Job 6:4, NIV). In Job 17:1, Job further cries: "My spirit is broken, my days are cut short, the grave awaits me" (NIV). Have you spent time in the desert lately thinking like Job? Most of us have and more of us will.

Desert times are normal testing times. Writing in his excellent book, *A Way through the Wilderness*, Jamie Buckingham says: "God's tests are learning experiences, designed by the Teacher to share knowledge, not to determine its presence or absence. . . . There are seasons when the man of God flourishes spiritually. Then there are times when the leaves of our life fall, the fruit disappears, and for all appearances our tree is lifeless. But each tree has a season, and in the proper season, the fruit reappears."[6]

Doorways to Dryness

Three conditions seem to lead us into seasons of desert dryness. First, we run dry when we are "stressed to the max"—emotional, mental, and physical exhaustion. Lack of proper diet and rest, overwork, interpersonal crises, career pressures, deadlines, health failure—any combination of these struggle points can sap you of vitality. Dryness results when you run out of gas and need time to refill your tank.

The second condition that brings us to a personal desert experience is when we grow tired and weary within our faith structure and run out of spiritual gas. Spiritual exhaustion prompts a disease called spiritual boredom. Once infected, we become critical, belligerent, indifferent, and callous. Jonah, Job, David, and Moses all suffered from this peculiar infection.

In Jonah 4, Jonah became critical of God's decision to spare the city of Ninevah. In a short space of time, Jonah moved from running from God to running back to God to running with God to trying to run ahead of God. In the end, he verbalized his indifference both to God and the people of Nineveh by uttering the words of a callous spirit; "It would be better for me to die than to live" (Jonah 4:8, NIV).

Job, although blessed with everything and then reduced to nothing, became critical of his own existence, belligerent to what God is trying to accomplish within him and indifferent to his friends who try to comfort him. Job's own hardened spirit prompts him to long for his own death (see Job 6:8, 9).

David knew success in his role as King of Israel. Perhaps it was spiritual boredom that caused him to become involved with Bathsheba. His embattled spirit, as he sought to recover from this encounter, is expressed best in Psalm 51.

Moses survived both a geographic and personal desert for 80 years of his life. From broken tablets to the complaints of his followers, Moses struggled with a critical and indifferent spirit much of the time.

Many people sitting in church pews today suffer from the same infections that plagued Jonah, Job, David, Moses and other great men of God. It is easy to identify with David when he proclaimed, "Restore unto me the joy of your salvation" (Psalm 51:12, NIV).

These two conditions that bring us to the spiritual desert could easily go under the headings "burned out" and "bored out." Both are natural and they will happen to all of us. The secret is to recognize when they are happening and take evasive action by getting apart and listening to God and letting Him take control of the situation. It is not easy to wait on God for we are taught to fix things in the quickest way possible. Waiting sometimes takes more energy and time than "quick-fixing."

The third condition that can put us in the desert of spiritual dryness is sin—disobeying God. We don't like to talk much about it, but sin short-circuits our relationship with the Lord and can induce the loneliest desert experiences of all. David wrote some of his psalms from the sin experiences in his life.

His words are plaintive cries for spiritual renewal and the restoration of God's presence in his life. It is only when sin is confessed and forgiveness is received that we experience restoration and renewal.

The Changing of the Seasons

Here's one final thought about enduring the inner desert experience. Most of us view it as an unproductive time in our lives rather than a time of incubation and inner growth. Christian productivity is a motivator in all of us. But we must realize that there will be times when little fruit appears on the vine of our life. The writer of Ecclesiastes tells us: "He makes all things beautiful in His time" (Ecclesiastes 3:11, NKJV). Everything is not beautiful and productive all the time. We have seasons in our lives, and Christian maturity should help us feel as comfortable with the seasons of planting and watering as with the seasons of fruitfulness. There is a time for the mountaintop and a time for the desert in our lives. Jamie Buckingham says:

> When your branches are barren, when your buds have dried up, when your leaves droop in discouragement, remember your roots. Remember that just beneath the sand there are underground reservoirs where the water is pure. Relax. Take your time. And know that in your season, you shall bear fruit again.[7]

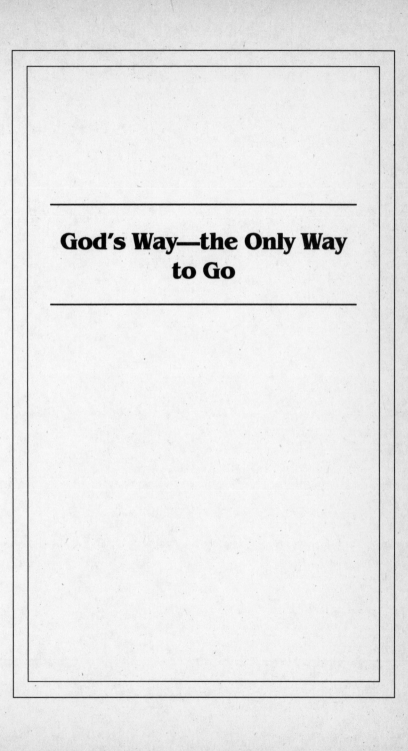

God's Way—the Only Way to Go

11

God's Way—the Only Way to Go

Many years ago, Charles M. Sheldon wrote a wonderful book titled *In His Steps* and subtitled *What Would Jesus Do?* The fictional story was about a church which decided to follow in Jesus' steps and, when faced with difficult situations in life, to ask the question, "What would Jesus do in this situation?" Church members desired to find God's answer to the question and not merely an expedient solution suggested by human desire or will.

Most of us have been on the Christian journey long enough to know that asking "What would Jesus do?" is seldom easy. In my own experience, I often fall into the category of the disciples when Jesus found them asleep in the garden: "The spirit is willing, but the body is weak" (Matthew 26:41, NIV). I always seem to have a willing spirit to do things God's way. And I know that the end result of any situation will be better if I follow the leading of the Lord at decision-making time. But I often have difficulty following through with waiting, watching, listening, and doing God's will even when my desire to do so is strong.

Doing things God's way is more of a process than an instant response. Since I am more acclimated to the instant, I tend to rush the process rather than wait for God's timing in matters. I am pushed by my own desire to see progress and by the cheers of those around me telling me to press ahead. I have a hard time realizing that God is never in a hurry and that I will do much better if I allow God to move on His timetable rather than squeeze Him into mine.

Part of my struggle is that it is more gratifying to see results than it is to wait for results. Waiting is usually a boring process in which little constructive gain seems to take place. Much of the time I spend in airports is waiting time. I look around at hundreds of other waiters who appear to be doing three things while waiting—eating, reading, or staring. All three seem prompted by the boredom of waiting. Action and progress lie at the other end of the plane flight, not at this end.

The classic biblical example of waiting is the 40 years Israel spent in the wilderness. I am sure that after the first three days of the journey most of them were ready to turn back. After 40 years of processing, they were allowed to leave the desert. And even then some had not learned the lessons God intended.

Israel waited 40 years.

Waiting for God's Way

Doing things God's way always starts with the process of waiting. That waiting includes waiting *before* the Lord, spending time with Him listening for His guidance and direction. It also means waiting *for* the Lord to do things in His way and on His time schedule. I come *before* Him and then I wait *for* Him. It is simple to understand yet hard to act upon. I often impatiently tell God, "Don't worry, Lord. I'll take care of it"—to which God must respond, "I'm sure you will!"

In Psalm 37:7, the psalmist tells us to, "Rest in the LORD, and wait patiently for Him; fret not yourself because of him who prospers in his way, because of the man who carries out wicked schemes" (NASB). Some of our reason for not waiting for the Lord lies in the second part of this verse. We are afraid that while we are waiting, someone else will get ahead of us on the road to prosperity, success, or whatever. While I am waiting, others may be doing and I will look silly and spiritually incompetent by comparison. Many people hastily do something and seek God's blessing on it later or take the blessing for granted. Worse still, they do something and tell everyone God told them to do it. There is a big difference between God getting the credit and God getting the blame.

great.

great guide for Church Growth

As I travel throughout the Christian community, the theme seems to be growth, action, progress, and motion. That's not a bad theme—unless its origin is more human than divine. We not only need to ask "Is God in this?" for our individual lives but also for activities in the family of God. Spiritual discernment is often replaced by the thrill of religious progress. Waiting for God's design and direction in our personal and corporate Christian journeys appears to be outmoded and archaic in a world of growth and mobility. Yet I wonder how much more of lasting gain would be accomplished if we would heed the psalmist's direction to wait.

The Art of Listening

You may be wondering, "What do I do while waiting for the direction of the Lord in my life?" The psalmist tells us to rest, which is a good admonition. I want to add another one of great importance: listen!

Listening is a lost art in today's world of rapid communication. Everyone seems to be talking; very few seem to be listening. Most of all, we do not listen to each other with the ears of our heart. We fail to hear the quiet inner cries and emotions that often cannot be articulated verbally. We perceive these messages by "listening" to moods, attitudes, and body language. We can only minister to one another in God's family if we listen to the sounds from the heart.

Listening to God also means listening to the sounds from His heart to our heart. It is allowing God to place His thoughts and His directions inside our heart much like He did to young Samuel in the Scriptures. The boy was called by a voice thought to come from a human source. But his human mentor Eli discerned that Samuel heard the call of God and said to him, "It is the LORD; let Him do what seems good to Him" (1 Samuel 3:18, NASB).

God will place His thoughts and directions within us if we

Rest + Listen while waiting

will but listen. To insure good direction, we are to evaluate God's inner voice by what Scripture teaches. God speaks with a soundness that will not betray what Scripture teaches.

We also need to be listening to fellow believers. God works as He has always worked, in and through His people. God used Eli to verify His calling of Samuel. God will often use trusted Christian friends and teachers to do the same for you and me if we are receptive. Those who walk closest to us are those who pray for us and who can often verify what God is saying to us. If you feel God is speaking to you, share what you are hearing with your closest Christian friends. If they cannot verify God's calling or direction, I caution you to wait longer and continue to pray. Remember, God is not in a hurry.

Listening to God is most often a private process. It is fine-tuning your spiritual ear to the inner promptings and urgings of God's Spirit. Sometimes that will mean getting away from the daily routines in your life to concentrate on hearing His voice. This is why the Scripture says, "Be still and know that I am God" (Psalm 46:10, NKJV). Knowing thrives in stillness. Stillness precedes listening. Listening takes a receptive and quiet spirit.

Don't Forget to Follow Through

Doing things God's way starts with waiting and listening. It continues by receiving and following the directions God gives, much like we follow the doctor's orders after an illness has been diagnosed. The struggle lies in the will to obey and receive the rewards of the obedience.

As we view the panorama of biblical characters parading, and sometimes stumbling, through Scripture, one truth is clear. They all received their directions intact, but when they failed in life it was due to their negligence in obeying God's instructions. And we also know the sad results of hearing God speak and failing to follow through obediently on His directives.

Obedience is easy for any of us because it means giving up our own will and giving in to God's will. The humbling process is often long and slow for each of us.

Doing things God's way does mean following His directions obediently. It also means allowing God to do things His way. And His way sometimes flies in the face of conventionality. It does not take much study of Scripture to discover that God often throws the predictable out the window when laying down His plan for us. Jesus constantly got in trouble both with secular and religious authorities because He refused to follow the established methods of behavior. He respected tradition yet He refused to allow it to rule people's lives.

The miraculous in our eyes is only ordinary and commonplace in God's eyes. I believe that God intends to operate in people's lives today the same way He did in biblical times. There are those who think God's way of doing things has changed since Jesus' earthly ministry and the beginnings of the early church. I believe such a view limits God much like the religious community did in Jesus' day. God defies the stereotypes we place upon Him and desires His freedom in our individual lives to do things His way.

Going His Way

Allowing God to have His way in our lives means understanding several things. First, God does not always follow predictable pathways in our lives. Many times, He does the unexpected in ways we think are impossible. Our personal astonishment at God's marvelous work sometimes comes later when we finally see how God tied many loose ends together to bring about His plan for us. Anticipating the unexpected from God brings us the joy of watching how God will bring things together for His glory and purpose. Rarely does God give us the entire game plan for something He is doing in our lives. He seems to keep us living on the edge so that we must trust Him to keep our balance. If we are to do things God's way, we must allow Him the freedom to do the unpredictable and the unexpected.

Second, God will seldom operate in your life the same way He operates in mine—and vice versa. Few of us seem to understand this. We tend to read the wonderful story of what God did in someone else's life and expect Him to duplicate the story in our lives. Some Christians are disappointed because they are told that God will do for them exactly what He has done for others if they only have faith to believe.

God is God, and He can break the mold if He so chooses. Our response to God's work in another's life should simply be, "Praise the Lord." He works His plan according to who we are and what we need, not on what has happened in someone else's life. Look at Jesus' healing ministry in the gospels, for example. Each event stood alone and different from any preceding it. What stayed the same was Jesus' feeling of compassion for the afflicted and His power to heal them. But His methodology was unique to the individual and the setting.

I have spent many years dealing with the divorce recovery process in people's lives. I always cringe when I hear someone tell an about-to-be-divorced person, "God put our marriage back together and, if He could do it for us, He can do it for you." I never doubt the "what God could do" part. But I know that it takes two people desiring restoration to make it happen. Since God gives us the right to make our own choices, some will make the wrong choice and some marriages will dissolve as a result.

If we could mandate God to heal all the broken relationships caused by divorce, we could also mandate God to heal the world from hunger, wars, crime, and all other human injustice. Since God did not make man as a robot, He does not force His will on us but allows us the freedom to make good and bad decisions. Our desire for God's will in our lives releases God to implement His unique plan for us.

No Need to Explain

Third, you need never to explain the "how" and the "why" of God's work in your life. We seem to spend an inordinate amount of time trying to explain to those around us what God is doing in us. I'm not sure if it's because we are unable to accept what God is doing or if we want others to cheer God for what He is doing. If we are going to allow God to be God, we must quit trying to explain His doings and simply stand in awe and reverence at the results. When the walls of Jericho came tumbling down, it would have been difficult on the human level to explain how God did it. To Israel, the end results were what counted. The same should be true to you and me. The less we try to explain the "how" and "why" of God, the more free we will be to enjoy the end result. To stand in awe at what God is doing is to have a strong sense of silent reverence at His power and plan made real in our daily wanderings through life.

Fourth, don't worry about what others will think about what God is doing in your life. Analyzing judgments appear to abound in the Christian community. We criticize everything from theological systems to how wide the spaces should be in church parking lots. And there will always be opinions on our individual responses to God's unique plan in our lives.

Apart from verifying God's call and direction with trusted brothers and sisters, we must stick with God's plan in the face of unfounded criticism. Our lives are to be reflected in Him, not in the opinions of others. Weigh every comment and criticism carefully, but follow through with what you know to be God's will.

I need to insert a thought here on accountability lest you misinterpret my aim. We are to please God first and foremost, but we are also accountable for our actions to one another in the Christian community. Spiritual license is granted only to God to do in us as *He* pleases. We are not free to do what *we* please. When God is truly at work in us, our actions and intents will seldom need explanation to those around us who really know God.

Finally, God's way is the way of adventure and challenge. There is nothing boring about following God. There is always the thrill of wondering how God will accomplish His purposes in our lives. To see God at work encourages us to be totally open and free to let Him do things His way. So God says to you and me, "Are you willing to let me take control?" And the best answer we can give is, "Yes, let's go!"

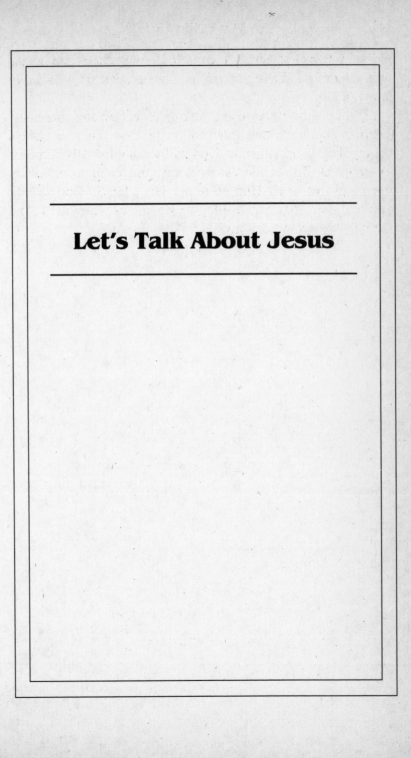

Let's Talk About Jesus

12

Let's Talk About Jesus

How many times in the past week have you talked about God in a warm and personal way with a fellow Christian? From my experience, Christians rarely hold conversations of that type. We tend to talk *around* God rather than *about* Him. Or we talk about God in a rather depersonalized and professional way. We seem to lack the freedom to talk about God to one another in simple and life-related ways. I often wonder how many spiritual conversations are generated by the Sunday sermon each week. It is easier to critique a sermon than it is to talk about the God at the center of it.

Perhaps our struggle with God-centered conversation is that we have so compartmentalized our faith that we can no longer talk about it with freedom and spontaneity. God can only become personal when we talk about Him to others in a personal way. Some would argue that a relationship with God is a private matter of the heart and soul and should not be discussed as one would talk of news, sports, and weather. This kind of thinking, though, does not follow biblical teaching and example. In the Old Testament, God was not locked away in the temple. He was a daily part of Israel's life and was talked about, as well as talked to, quite freely. In the times of the gospels and the early church people talked openly and often about God to each other. God was viewed as personally present and powerfully active in the lives of His people.

What has happened to our freedom to talk about God with one another? One of the inhibitors to this kind of sharing is the fear that we don't know enough about God to talk about Him, and if we attempt to we will appear spiritually inadequate. A second excuse for our lack of God-talk is that we don't want to be seen as super-spiritual. We are easily turned off by the spiritual mumbo jumbo that some people employ to gain a one-up on Christians around them. A third reason stems from our inability to know what to say when talking about God to our friends. We try to find the balance between spiritual inadequacy and super-spirituality, only to find our mouths open with nothing coming out.

How to Start Talking

Conversations about God with our friends can start with simple questions such as, "What is God saying in your life right now?" and "What is God doing in your life right now?" These questions are door-openers to deeper discussion about the workings of God in our personal lives. Many of us would answer "I'm not sure" to the above questions at any given time. And that kind of answer should open the door to personal exploration together rather than close it for fear we cannot read the signposts and signals in our life. Too often we want to express comprehensive answers so that we will appear spiritually confident. In reality, one question can lead to further questions and greater growth. God is not the God of the answered question. He is the God of the open question and the ongoing expression of His direction in our lives. We tend to reach for finalization while God reaches for openness and process.

Speaking Professionally

Many of us fall into the trap of talking professionally about God to one another. Professional conversations usually include all the Christian events we have attended, all the Christian people we know, all the Christian activities we have accomplished, and the latest gossip from within the Christian community. To many, the Christian world is clearly defined and we talk within its confines with ease and safety. We even add to this framework a vocabulary of Christian terms. These words have slightly different meanings depending on which Christian circle they are spoken in.

One bedraggled and battered word that is often loosely used is "blessing." Everything in the Christian community seems to fit under this banner. It is probably the most generic Christian word around. Its definition can run anywhere from mediocre to stupendous. What is a blessing to you may be far short of a blessing to someone else. Sometimes the bigger the event and the larger the numbers, the greater the blessing we are supposed to receive. We need to rethink some of our "Christianese" language and how we use it.

It is relatively safe to talk professionally about God. Since we are talking objectively instead of subjectively, we need never fear talking about our personal walk and struggles with God. Frankly, I'm very weary of professional God talk. I desire the freedom to talk with others about God in a personal way. It is time we talked to each other about our inner journeys with the Lord in openness and honesty. It is time we had the freedom to say we are doing well or not doing well spiritually and to explore the many questions and feelings we have about God. It is also time that we quit assuming everyone is doing well spiritually. Spiritual silence does not necessarily mean spiritual progress. It may well mean struggle and doubt in one's life.

Tell It As It Is

Another recently emerging tendency in talking about God involves talking only about great victories and triumphs in one's life. I have yet to see anyone invited to appear on a Christian talk show who does not have a victorious testimony of a spiritual triumph to share with the viewers. Wouldn't it be helpful to hear a story of personal struggle with no victory yet in sight? God is not only the author of the happy ending story. He is also the author of the continuing struggle story. The danger of listening to all the happy ending stories is in believing that you are not a victorious Christian without numerous mountain top victories to share. God gives victories. Of that there is no doubt. God enacts miracles in lives for certain. But it is also okay to talk about our in-process miracles before the happy ending scene. In fact, perhaps the solution to our struggles will come sooner if we talk through them and pray about them with other believers.

My Jesus

Still another side of talking about God is the possessional side, or what I call "hugging Jesus to yourself." God is talked about as a personal possession rather than the God who is active in the lives of all believers. The words "accept Jesus as your personal Savior" have boomeranged on many of today's Christians. Jesus is not a possession to be guarded and hoarded. He is the Lord of the universe to be shared with others. It is possible that we talk about Jesus in such exclusive terms that others feel excluded from Him. There is no mention of this kind of exclusive faith anywhere in the Scriptures. Perhaps it reflects the battle among the disciples to see who would sit closest to Jesus in the kingdom. Maybe we are still fighting the battle to see who is closest to Him today.

Let's Get Practical

We've talked about how not to talk about God. If there is one word to describe how we should talk, it is practical. God is the God of the practical and we can talk openly and practically about Him with our brothers and sisters. We are free to ask our many questions about God to one another and raise our many doubts as well.

Along with the questions, doubts, and struggles we have

with God, there is also the need to celebrate God's nature and activity openly with one another. A vital part of the practical God-talk is knowing what God has done in others' lives in times past. Whenever the great leaders in Scripture were met with an insurmountable challenge, they reminded the people of what God had done for them in their past. They had an established history with God, and that history was a foundation for their tomorrows. We need to talk to our friends about what God has done in our yesterdays in order to encourage one another for our todays and tomorrows.

Scriptural promises are another topic for conversation. They are there to affirm that God will do what He has stated. Talking with our friends about God means reminding them of God's promises for our lives.

Talking practically with our friends about God allows us to share feelings and emotions about God with one another. Biblical characters were often emotionally expressive to one another about God. Our world today has tended to inhibit us from outward expressions about God. We are free to talk about our feelings because God equipped us with feelings and they are integral to our Christian experiences. We have joyful moments with God to share as well as moments of anger, sadness and doubt. We need to talk about all these topics with friends in God's family.

It is not easy to begin open discussion about God with one another. But ordinary Christians will take the risk!

[illegible] part of the year will [illegible]

[illegible]

[illegible] and they [illegible] all these forces [illegible]

[illegible]

Giving God Space at the Center

13

Giving God Space at the Center

Continually discover God at the center of your being so that you can carry Him into the midst of your doing.[1]

There are two lingering maladies in the life of the Christian today: cluttered lives and scattered attention. We are batted between the two like the proverbial ping-pong ball as we try to make sense out of our daily existence. Somewhere between the clutter and the scatter, we try to give God some space so we can carry on for one more day. What generally happens is that God gets His space on Sunday morning or whenever we are hit with a crisis that is bigger than we are. For many of today's Christians, the stretch between Sunday mornings and crises becomes a spiritual wasteland where God is rarely acknowledged.

The Battle for Space

Most of us have compartmentalized our cluttered lives into several areas. There is people space, home space, work space, church space, schedule space, and personal space. For the most part, God is slotted into the church space while the other areas are full of our daily doing. With all the other spaces crying out for our attention, it is little wonder that God gets squeezed out of our daily activities and confined only to the devotional compartments in our lives.

The struggle for economic survival in society gives strong priority to the work space. In many homes both husband and wife work eight- to ten-hour days and then struggle to cram the essentials of life into the little time that is left over. Finding time for the important is like an impossible dream for too many of us.

It is easy to live for hours, days, and even weeks with our only thought of God tucked between the pages of our daily devotional guide. We are living examples of the bumper sticker which reads, "If you feel far away from God, guess who moved." We find ourselves craving the freedom of a spiritual simplicity that would allow God to fill the spaces of our lives with His presence. Many Christians find themselves envious of their ministers who can spend their days with the comings and goings of God in their work. Yet pastors repeatedly tell me that their lives are full of busy work and that even their work often has too little of God in it. Christians and laypeople alike have become all too professional with their faith. We have neatly filed God somewhere between our desire and our dreams in our journey.

Although God seems to go begging for personal space in our lives, He does occupy a lot of shelf space today. God has never been more popular in our society than He today. We attest to His importance by purchasing and displaying "God momentos" in our homes, offices, and automobiles, around our necks, and on our lapels. We Christians have become walking billboards for the popularity of God. He is addressed before city council meetings, sessions of our government, classrooms in schools, football games, etc. The words "born again," which came to public prominence during the Jimmy Carter presidency, have been tied to anyone and anything that involves a change or new beginning. Christian jargon has never been more popular or widely used.

God as a commodity has never before experienced the kind of human popularity that He does today. He occupies more space on our shelves but increasingly less space in our hearts. The words Paul wrote to Timothy should bring us up short: "People will be . . . lovers of pleasure rather than lovers of God—having a form of godliness but denying its power. Have nothing to do with them" (2 Timothy 3:2,4,5, NIV).

The greatest danger we all face in this area is following the form but denying the power. It is one thing to have an identity *with* the Lord. It is quite another thing to have our identity *within* the Lord. There is nothing wrong with the many outward expressions of our identity with God's family. The problem comes when these expressions become the standard for our identity with God. It's like wearing a football uniform everywhere you go but never playing the game. You would look like a football player to everyone, but you would not know the joy of really participating in the sport. If someone asked, "Do you enjoy football?," you would have to respond, "I never played the game!" Ordinary Christians get in the game. They don't just wear the uniform.

Developing God Awareness

Let me suggest four ways that might help us give God the space He deserves in our lives. The first is to develop what I call God awareness—having the understanding that God walks with me in all the areas of my life each day. God awareness is consciously acknowledging that He is present in every place I find myself. Jesus promised His followers, "And surely I will be with you always, to the very end of the age" (Matthew 28:20, NIV). On the strength of His promise I need to constantly affirm, "God is right here with me."

Affirming His presence is acknowledging our awareness of Him. His Spirit is with us in supermarkets, board rooms, service stations, freeways, conversations, struggles, etc. It is being aware that when God is with us, we are standing on holy ground. Holy ground is not only the place of pews and stained glass. It is any place where the Lord is with us and we are aware of Him. For me, I need to focus intently on that as I go about my daily journey. And that awareness is not just based upon feeling. There are some times I feel very alone in my humanness, but that does not mean God is not present. Consciously, I must say, "You are right here, Lord." If I know that God is right with me, I won't need to worry about Him finding me or catching up with me.

I have also discovered that I respond to situations differently if I am aware of God's presence. Too many of us do whatever we want because we believe that God is not around at the moment. A direct and concentrated awareness of Him will prevent such thoughtless behavior.

Practicing God's Presence

The second way to give God space in our lives is closely akin to the first: practicing His presence in all areas of our daily walk. This discipline describes building a constant fellowship with God much as we would desire to build human friendship.

A book that has become a spiritual classic, *Practicing His Presence* by Brother Lawrence and Frank Laubach, gives positive direction in this area. Concerning practicing Christ's presence in our lives, Laubach says: "Experience has told us that good resolutions are not enough. We need to discipline our lives in an ordered regimen. So many of us have found the idea of turning to Christ once every minute to be enormously helpful. It is a practice as old as Enoch, who 'walked with God.' It is a way of living which nearly everybody knows and nearly everybody has ignored. It is a delightful experience and an exhilarating spiritual exercise; but we will soon discover that it is far more than even that. Some people have compared it to getting out of a dark prison and beginning to live. We still see the same world, yet it is not the same, for it has a new, glorious color and a far deeper meaning."[2]

Laubach states that he started this minute-to-minute practicing of God's presence by "trying to line up my actions with the will of God about every fifteen minutes or every half hour."[3] Most of us would fall far short of doing so once a week. We excuse ourselves by stating we are too busy with our everyday priorities to move toward a more God-centered life. We feel this minute-by-minute approach is a discipline for full-time religious professionals in our midst, but not for us.

In Psalm 27:8, David exclaims, "When You said, 'Seek My face,' my heart said to You, 'Your face, Lord, I will seek' " (NKJV). David's desire was to live in full view of the Lord. He knew God's presence had to fill his life if he was to survive his daily journey. He knew the experience of living without God and of living fully before Him, openly attentive to Him.

Does the minute-to-minute approach discourage you? Let me suggest you spend some time thinking about how you can bring Christ's presence into your daily life in a more direct way. It takes thoughtful discipline, and it can be done without stopping everything else you are doing. We drive a car with a stick shift through the tangles of traffic each day and never think about the shifting process. It's second nature to us. We can do the same by consciously working on the areas of our life where Christ desires access and control. The things we desire most come through the process of discipline. Our thoughts form the needs and desires of our hearts. Daily discipline brings them into observance.

Brother Lawrence states, "I cannot imagine how a Christian can live a satisfied Christian experience without the practice of being in the presence of Christ. For my part, I keep myself retired with Him in the center of my soul as much as I can. While I am with Him, I fear nothing. Even the slightest turning away from Him on my part is indefensible."[4] When we move into His presence, our relationship with the Lord grows. When we stay outside of Him, our relationship fades and our power to live for Him diminishes.

Few of us today would deny that we need to practice the awareness of His presence more effectively in our lives. The consequence of not doing so can be similar to that of Jonah when he "ran away from the LORD" (Jon. 1:3, NIV). We may not be swallowed by a great fish, but we will be consumed by the emptiness that robs our Christian life of real joy and meaning. This same emptiness leads to boredom in our Christian journey and a growing desire to find spiritual gimmicks to take the place of Christ's daily, active presence in our lives.

Tapping into God's Power

The third way that we can give God space in our lives is to allow His power to become our power. In the pre-birth moments of the early church, the disciples were instructed to wait for the promise of the Father. The promise in Acts 1:8 was that they would receive power when the Holy Spirit had come upon them and that power would enable them to be Christ's witnesses throughout the entire earth. They were not to meet the world without the new power that Christ would give them, nor could they be sustained without it. The record of the book of Acts bears this out.

One of our struggles today in the Christian community seems to be the lack of God's power in our Christian experience. When we do in our own strength what should be done by God's power, we run the risk of creating the mechanical rather than the miraculous. Although fired with zeal after Jesus left them, the disciples were commanded to coolly await God's power for their mission. They were not to operate on human strength and ingenuity. They were not to build an explainable kingdom of God. They were to build the miraculous kingdom of God. They possessed practical training and knowledge from the years they had spent with Jesus. But they needed the infusion of His power. Once the Spirit came, they would know that He was the only source of their power.

It is easy to operate on your own energy, knowledge, intellect, and abilities. And all those elements are gifts from God and should not be negated or denied. They are only useful in

God's eyes, however, when they are plugged into the source that makes them operable—God's power.

We only get into trouble when we seek to operate unplugged from God's power. His power is not given to impress but to implement. God's power was never intended to be a fireworks show in the Christian's walk with God. Too often it has become that to many Christians. Even Jesus resisted the show of power when Satan tempted Him in the desert. Jesus knew that real power from His heavenly Father did not need public display to prove its existence.

Our whole world today is structured around power systems. There are those who have it, those who desire it, and those who fear it. We all fall into each of those categories at different times. Kingdoms rise and fall today under the baton of power. The power that God desires to give us is far removed from the self-consuming power the world desires. His power is given that we might have the ability to do what He wants us to do. God's power is never self-consuming; it is always self-abasing. Paul's desire was to know Christ's resurrection power. Resurrection power is the power of personal transformation that occurs through personal surrender to Christ. It was power for personal change that Paul sought, not power for display purposes.

We invite God to take His rightful space in our lives. He comes equipped with power. It is His desire to infuse us with that power so we can live to the praise of His glory. It is also His desire to equip us with His power so we can do His works. Without His power, we can only do our own works. But with His power, we can do what He intended for us to do. In order to be available for God's power in my life, I must be willing to relinquish the exercise of my own power—not an easy task since power gives me a feeling of control, value, esteem, and authority. The words of the prophet Zechariah haunt me here: " 'Not by might nor by power, but by my Spirit,' says the LORD Almighty" (Zechariah 4:6, NIV). Any power I have is the power of personal might. God's power is Spirit power. I must switch off my own power and switch on God's power in its place.

There is little question that the ordinary Christians who populated the pages of Scripture were receptive to the power of God in their lives. That same power is available to you and me today. Without it, we will personify the biggest power failure the world has ever witnessed.

Becoming God-centered

The fourth way of giving God space in our lives deals with becoming God-centered. In order for me to become God-centered, I must first move everything out of the center of my life that doesn't belong there—namely myself, my goals, my priorities, and my preferences. God is not vying for space in a back corner of our lives. He is asking to be at the center of our lives. If we want God to take His place within us we must offer Him the center. The problem is that the center and fringes of our lives are often clogged and cluttered with many activities and pursuits which displace Christ and thwart what He would bring to us.

Some of us have placed the stuff of life in the center and surrounded it with the things of God. This leaves God at the edges rather than at the center. Better we place Christ at the center and let everything else gather around Him. Perhaps this is why Jesus said, "But I, when I am lifted up from the earth, will draw all men to myself" (John 12:32, NIV). Christ must be seen at the center in order to draw people to Himself.

Have you made space for God at the center of your life? Or do you still have Him neatly tucked away in a room called "Sunday" or standing around the corner from a place called "Personal Crisis"?

Just as we need to have our center in Christ, Christ must be at the center of us. If you are willing to give God space, make sure it is center space!

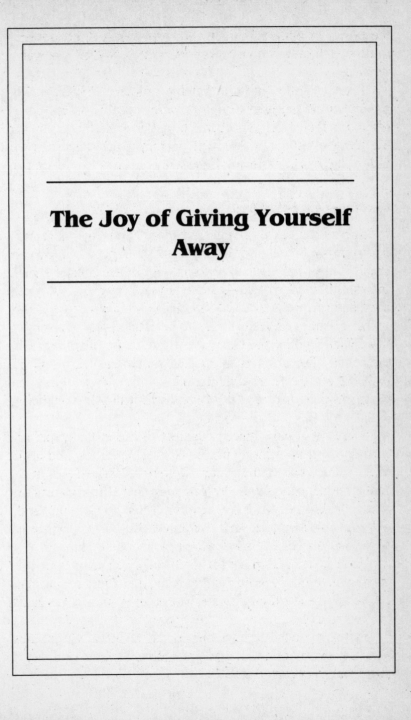

The Joy of Giving Yourself Away

14

The Joy of Giving Yourself Away

> As each one has received a gift, minister it to one another, as good stewards of the manifold grace of God. (1 Peter 4:10, NKJV).

Little is more exciting and gratifying than giving and receiving gifts. We look forward to the special times when we can share in the warmth of this unique experience. Some of us would rather give gifts than receive them while others enjoy receiving more than giving. Whichever side you are on, you doubtless know the joy of exchanging gifts.

It should cause little wonder that God understands our joy at giving and receiving, for He introduced spiritual gifts to the family of God. The discovery and utilization of spiritual gifts within the Christian community has almost become a lost teaching in the church today. Most Christians know that spiritual gifts are mentioned somewhere in Scripture but don't have a clue for relating them to their own lives.

Few people in our churches are selected for tasks based on their spiritual gifts. Many Christians are driven into service by guilt, default, or desire rather than their spiritual qualifications. Consequently, many find themselves failing in areas of Christian service because they lack God-given skills for their roles. Even professional Christian leaders struggle to fulfill ministry obligations for which they have no spiritual giftedness. New church members are urged into service with little or no discussion of their giftedness. The business world does a far better job of matching people to jobs that fit their innate abilities.

Too many people in the church and the world flounder in

life-consuming tasks for which they are not gifted. The result is personal misery, depression, lack of productivity, restlessness, and constant flitting from task to task looking for affirmation. After about 30 years of observing Christians in the church, I estimate that about 80 percent are involved in tasks that they are simply not gifted to perform. Many are plodding through a term of service praying for a side door to spring open so they can escape. Often that side door is blocked by a well-meaning pastor who is more concerned with filling holes than discovering gifts.

What Are Gifts All About?

There is clear teaching in Scripture about spiritual gifts and their purpose. The basic guidelines are spelled out in Romans 12:1–8; Ephesians 4:11–13; 1 Corinthians 12:1–11; and 1 Peter 4:10,11. Peter Wagner defines spiritual gifts in this way: "A spiritual gift is a special attribute given by the Holy Spirit to every member of the Body of Christ according to God's grace for use within the context of the Body."[1] The Scripture teaches (and Wagner's definition summarizes) who gives the gift, why the gift is given, and where the gift is to be employed. If we implemented the Scriptural teaching of spiritual gifts within the Christian community, we would create harmony and great productivity in ministry. People would be set free from desiring someone else's gift and challenged to see their own gift as special and useable in the family of God. We would also be equipped to say no when asked to do something we are not gifted to do.

It is God's desire and design that Christians work together efficiently and smoothly within His family. Disharmony usually results from doing what one is not gifted to do. Happiness comes from discovering and utilizing one's gift.

Wagner identifies 27 spiritual gifts from his study of Scripture: prophecy, service, teaching, exhortation, giving, leadership, mercy, wisdom, knowledge, faith, healing, miracles, discerning of spirits, tongues, interpretation of tongues, apostles, helps, administration, evangelist, pastor, celibacy, voluntary poverty, martyrdom, hospitality, missionary, intercession, and exorcism.

I am sure as you look at the list there are some gifts you wish you had and some you hope you never have—such as the gift of martyrdom!

Are Some Gifts Better?

One of the major confrontations in Paul's ministry was over which gifts were most important. This argument within the church at Corinth led Paul to write the Love chapter—1 Corinthians 13—and stress love as the all-important and all-consuming gift for every believer.

Conflicts over the preference of spiritual gifts still arise today. The gifts of strength and showiness—such as teaching and leadership—are often more desirable to us than the quiet gifts of mercy and helps. The gifts of miracles and healing would certainly be in greater demand in the average Christian community than those of celibacy and poverty. Where spiritual gifts are acknowledged and taught today, there are always a few people who desire the more showy gifts that will put them in front of the rest.

In some Christian circles, the more spectacular gifts—for example, healing, miracles, tongues, and exorcism—have been relegated to the days of the apostles and the early church, after which they supposedly passed into obscurity. If you eliminate a gift, you apparently eliminate the controversy of its use. More and more Christians believe today that all the gifts in Scripture are still to be in operation within the body of Christ. Ordinary Christians look upon spiritual gifts as God's way of equipping them to minister to one another within the Christian community so that the community may be strong.

Someone once told me that a gift is not a gift until it is given to someone. I think that is a good way to view our spiritual gifts. A spiritual gift is of little value when it is hidden within you. Released in the community, your gift can aid in the growth and maturity of other believers. The gifts listed in Ephesians 4:11 were given to equip the saints for ministry and to edify the Body of Christ. They were not given to be possessed or paraded. They were given to be practiced and productive.

As you look around the community of your Christian friends, how many spiritual gifts can you identify in others? How many of those gifts are really being used to build up your group? Chances are good that most of your Christian friends cannot even identify their gifts let alone understand how they should be employed in ministry. It was only after being in ministry for a number of years that I came to grips with my own spiritual gifts. I thought I had some I really did not have and wanted others I knew I did not have. My primary gift is exhortation. When I go to the hospital I wish my gift was healing, but it isn't. It is my responsibility to perfect and hone my gift of exhortation and not move into areas in which I am not gifted.

I have always wished that I was gifted in fixing things. I envy others who can. The best I can do is make sure I have a few friends around me who have that ability. At the heart of any good friendship is the exchange of gifts. God understood that when He gave us spiritual gifts. Our relationships deepen and are nourished in the administration of those gifts to one another.

What About My Gifts?

The two primary questions in discovering and developing your spiritual gifts are, "How do I identify my gifts?" and "How and when do I utilize them?" Peter Wagner says there are four fundamental prerequisites in finding your gift or gifts. First, you have to be a Christian since spiritual gifts are given only to members of the Body of Christ. Second, you have to believe in spiritual gifts. Many who don't believe in them simply have not been taught. Third, you have to be willing to work. The exercising of spiritual gifts is a job which must be worked at. Fourth, you have to pray. Wagner elaborates on the many processes involved in the unveiling of spiritual gifts. I recommend that you purchase and read the book.

One key responsibility we have to one another in discovering our spiritual gifts is what I call the "calling forth" of the gifts we see in one another. We often do not see our own gift when it is staring us in the face, but it may be quite obvious to our closest friends. We help one another in this area by telling them what we see and feel, and by helping them develop or call forth their gift. God often operates in our lives through others. When God enables us to identify a gift in a brother or sister, He also enables us to encourage that gift to be used. This is no different than recognizing physical talents in others and prompting them to use those talents for the good of all.

The calling forth of the spiritual gifts we see in others is also an affirmation that God loves us and allows us to minister to one another through our giftedness. There are tremendous needs within the family of God today. Many Christians are dying a slow spiritual death because there is no one ministering to them through the avenue of biblical spiritual gifts. People need healing, both physically and mentally, yet few seem to exercise the gift of healing. We need wisdom for the many decisions we face in daily life, yet there seem to be so few around us with the gift of wisdom to be shared. We wage a constant battle with the forces of evil in our life, but we look far and long for someone with the gift of discerning the spirits. We struggle with our faith on the waters of life, but can seldom find a friend with the spiritual gift of strong faith.

Why Don't We Give?

We usually see evidence of only a few of the spiritual gifts today, the most noticeable being hospitality, helps, service, and teaching. These gifts tend to be relatively safe and more practical than many of the others. Filed away under "Obscure" are gifts like intercession, exorcism, celibacy, and voluntary poverty. Filed under "Divisive" are the gifts of tongues, miracles, prophecy, and healing. Elevated to the speaker's platform are the gifts of pastor, missionary, evangelist, and leadership.

Gift rejection seems like more of a problem among us than gift selection. Could it be that we resist certain gifts because they might prove embarrassing to us or our churches? I believe that God knows more about what we can handle gift-wise than we do. Our fear can keep our gifts from being affirmed and used by God in community.

Discovering your spiritual gift is both a process and an adventure. Perfecting and exercising your spiritual gift is a lifetime commitment. It is closely akin to developing athletic ability. It takes time, patience, and practice. Once you have developed a skill, it never totally goes away. And the more you use it, the more proficient you will become. Lack of use leads to abuse.

Spiritual gifts are to be used within the Christian community. They are designed to build up the family of God by building up its members. When spiritual gifts are not in evidence, the Body of Christ becomes weak and ineffective. Its members will not grow when gifts are not shared.

How to Give Yourself Away

Spiritual gifts can be shared in two basic ways—corporately and individually. Corporate sharing is when the gift is utilized within the context of a group structure such as a worship service. Gifts may be directed at the entire group or one or more persons within the group. Leadership is an example of a corporately shared gift. Service, teaching, and exhortation may also be corporately expressed. Individually shared gifts could be intercession, wisdom, helps, giving, and healing.

As with any gift, spiritual gifts need a giver and a receiver. If all the receivers want to be givers, the gift is negated—and vice versa. Many of us feel that being on the receiving end obligates us to reciprocate. Spiritual gifts, however, are to be given and received freely. We are not to keep account, but simply give thanks to God the ultimate giver.

You and I are ordinary Christians who have been given extraordinary spiritual gifts. We are not to keep them under wraps. Instead we should acknowledge them, be responsible for them, be responsive to them, and use them for the common good of the Body of Christ. Paul states: "But the manifestation of the Spirit is given to each one for the profit of all" (1 Corinthians 12:7, NKJV). Gifts can be self-consuming if they are not used for others.

Since there is often much confusion on the topic of spiritual gifts, you would do well to spend time studying the Scriptural passages listed in this chapter and read the definitions at the end of Peter Wagner's book, *Your Spiritual Gifts Can Help Your Church Grow*.

God never intended for us as believers to live the Christian experience without equipment. We are given spiritual gifts, spiritual armor, and fruits of the Spirit that we might "grow in grace." The elements we need have already been planted. We are to assure their growth by allowing the Holy Spirit to bring them to maturity.

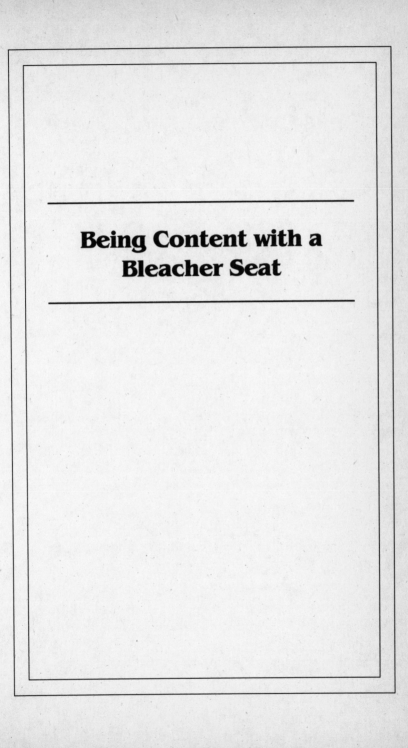

Being Content with a Bleacher Seat

15

Being Content with a Bleacher Seat

Have you ever sat so far away from the action on a baseball field that you would have had a better view in front of your television set at home? You squint in the sunlight from the far reaches of the left-field stands and notice that there are a host of people sitting right behind home plate—the best seats in the stadium. You confess to a great deal of envy and wish that you were important enough to own season tickets to those select quarters. Often it is the rich, famous, and very important people in our world who occupy those seats. Many of us "bleacher bums" would give a lot to sit where those people sit. They have the best of the best and we look upon them with envy.

The ordinary Christian and the ordinary baseball fan have a lot in common. Both seem to want conditions to be far better than they are. There is apparently little contentment in knowing that others have a better seat in the kingdom of God than you do. It may appear frivolous to equate secular striving with sacred striving, but the truth remains that many of today's Christians are looking to improve their position and status in the family of God. The quest for spiritual upward mobility is found among leaders as well as followers. Christian leaders, from my experience, want the same benefits from their positions that non-Christian leaders want. And Christian followers often crave the same advantages that the secular crowd desires.

To occupy the best position is indeed ego-enhancing. It is recognition, reward, acclaim, success, and a "Hey, look at me!" attitude all rolled in one. We are fighting the battle of the personal ego in the Christian community today as never before. The standards for success in the secular community have permeated the Christian community, and biblical standards for handling success and ego have fallen by the wayside.

Pursuing Prominence

Our attitudes are similar to those found in Mark 10:35, 45. "Then James and John, the sons of Zebedee, came to him. 'Teacher,' they said, 'we want you to do for us whatever we ask.' 'What do you want me to do for you?' he asked. They replied, 'Let one of us sit at your right and the other at your left in your glory' " (NIV).

On the surface, the request of James and John could be seen as nothing more than wanting to be close to Jesus because they loved Him. One could surmise that their goal was fellowship rather than status. And some Christians today use the same reasoning as they seek position in the Christian community. The real truth is that James and John, who along with Peter were closer to Jesus than the other disciples, really wanted to become Jesus' chief ministers of state when He set up His kingdom. They were in pursuit of power, success, identity, and importance. They wanted to be numbers two and three in the new kingdom. The seats to the left and right of Jesus would fulfill that desire.

Jesus did not chastise them directly for their desire, but He did ask them if they were willing to pay the price for their request. They eagerly agreed, not understanding that Jesus was referring to hardship and death. Then He told them that only the Father could grant their desire; it was not His place to give it.

It fascinates me that the story continues with the response from the other disciples when they heard what James and John were after. Mark 10:41 states: "When the ten heard about this, they became indignant with James and John" (NIV). We cannot be sure what provoked displeasure in the remaining disciples. It could have been that they felt "one-upped" by James and John and had lost their own personal chances at the prime seats. They may have been hurt to think any of their number would be so ambitious. Jealousy or sadness, we don't really know. But we do know that followers of Christ were as human then as they are today in their desire for place and position in the Christian community.

We should be motivated by the love of Christ and our desire to do His will in all things. Power, status, authority, and prominence are never to be the goal of the Christian. Jesus taught submission, servanthood, service, and giving preference to others rather than to ourselves. He said that the way to any crown we may ultimately receive was through the cross that we bear. Crowns are awarded for submissive humility rather than star-studded humanity.

Position by Association

We not only struggle with the desire for personal fame and power, by we also wrestle with the desire for importance gained from association with those who already have it. I will never forget the night I sat just a few rows away from a famous Hollywood actor at a ball game. I never said a word to him but I sure told all my friends that I was near him. I even look closely at the people sitting in first-class when I fly so I can tell others if someone important was on my last flight.

It is easy to derive one's own sense of importance from being close to those who are important. I am sure the disciples wanted everyone to know that they were with Jesus when He performed miracles. But they were strangely absent when the pressures of His trial, imprisonment, and crucifixion took place. They wanted the notoriety of association with Jesus until the going got tough.

Our desire to be close to those of importance has given rise to the star system within the Christian community today. We elevate Christian leaders to guru status, follow their every move, and heed their every word in order to be esteemed as a disciple of a famous Christian. We drift into the controversy that Paul faced with the Corinthian Christians when they started aligning themselves with either Paul, Apollos, or Cephas (see 1 Corinthians 1:11,12). Paul's corrective admonition to them was simply put: "I planted the seed, Apollos watered it, but God made it grow" (1 Corinthians 2:6, NIV). Paul did not deny the capabilities of those in Christian leadership. But he did urge the Corinthians to correct their course and seek only to glorify God. Anyone who ministered to them was simply a servant who was used by God as a part of their growth. God's servants can be appreciated but they are not to be placed on a pedestal.

Problems with Pedestals

We humans seem to be born pedestal builders. Some of us build our own pedestals and install ourselves on top of them. Others are elevated to pedestals which adoring fans have built for them. Either way, God often knocks the pedestal out from under us to bring us back to ground level.

Some of the dangers we encounter with pedestal people is in what they say. Since many notable Christian leaders disagree on Christian doctrine and practice, you begin to wonder whose teaching is right and whose is wrong. Or we wonder who is closest to the real truth because we want to follow that person rather than others who are not as close to the truth.

Sometimes our evaluation of pedestal people centers on who is rated highest in the Christian world. Just as we want our favorite baseball team in first place, so we want our pet pedestal person in first place.

We also have an insatiable desire to elevate new pedestal people in our lives. We look for the newest and most promising rising star to identify with. We also watch for those who are in decline and disfavor in Christian community. We use and discard our pedestal people with increasing frequency. Few of them stay around as long as Moses did. Moses' longevity was based on a call from God. Many of today's leaders follow a call based on personal popularity rather than on divine mandate.

A final phenomenon of the pedestal people syndrome is the way those on pedestals seem intent on cloning themselves in others. Unfortunately, the call from the pedestal to "follow me" conflicts with God's call to "follow Me." There is an authentic call from God for leadership in the Christian community. The struggle lies in how leaders handle that call and how they allow their followers to handle that call. Leaders should be respected but not cloned. Only God can make a true leader.

Ordinary Christians should highly esteem those whom God places in leadership positions within Christian community. But we should not tolerate those leaders who install themselves as pedestal people or Christian gurus. Our identity is not linked to our position or associations. Our identity is founded in who we are in Christ Jesus.

We have talked about the higher levels of leadership in the Christian community. We also need to say something about secondary levels such as members of committees, boards, and councils. The battles for position and personal association go from the top of the ladder down to the bottom. The lowliest committee formed to coordinate the raking of leaves in the fall can be filled with all the status-grabbing problems we have mentioned to this point. The struggle for power and importance can be found on every level of Christian organization. It is even found in families. The battle for power and prominence has destroyed many once-healthy structures. It is only when a person submits to the control of Christ in his life that he can abdicate the struggle for eminence and dominance. God is not only the center of all power, but He deserves all the glory as well, which leads us to the place of praise as a result of leadership.

Deserving Praise

Praise or affirmation is a by-product of recognition and leadership. Some in leadership never seem to get enough of it. Like a famous celebrity once said, "I didn't know what to do when they finally stopped clapping for me." Praise can motivate and elevate a person in a positive manner. It can also inflate the ego to such proportions that constant injections of praise are needed to keep the person running. Too much praise convinces a person that he or she has succeeded by himself. It also has a way of putting God in second place and elevating the individual to first place. Many great biblical characters fell from leadership when personal pride and praise for accomplishment got in the way. I am reminded of the words of an old hymn by A.B. Simpson:

> Not I but Christ, be honored, loved, exalted;
> Not I but Christ, be seen, be known, be heard;
> Not I but Christ, in every look and action,
> Not I but Christ, in every thought and word.
> O to be saved from myself, dear Lord,
> O to be lost in Thee,
> O that it might be no more I,
> But Christ that lives in me.[1]

These powerful words are seldom sung in today's churches but they are as true for today's generation of Christians as for any in the past. Most of us need to be rescued from ourselves more than we need to be rescued from others. We need to know that Christ can take the place of the "I" in our lives.

Ordinary Christians know that when praise flows in their direction, God is the one who receives the credit. Perhaps a good response to praise is simply to say, "Praise the Lord." It can mean, "I don't care who gets the credit as long as God gets the glory."

Paul wrote some sober words about our personal self-concept:

> Do not think of yourself more highly than you ought, but rather think of yourself soberly with judgment, in accordance with the measure of faith God has given you (Romans 12:3, NIV).

James offered good advice also:

> Humble yourselves before the Lord, and he will lift you up" (James 4:10, NIV).

Hospital stays are a humbling experience

Being lifted to a higher plateau in our life will come through God's power if we walk humbly before Him. Godly exaltation is far more valuable than human exaltation or praise.

One of the best ways that you and I can deal with our desire for prominence, position, or praise is to realize that we are called to be servants with humble hearts. Identity and success within the Christian community cannot be handled the same way it is in secular community. There is no self-made man or woman in the family of God. We are what we are by His power. We must remember Jesus' words: "Apart from me you can do nothing" (John 15:5, NIV).

Ordinary Christians aren't looking for the best seat. But they are looking for God's place for them!

Epilogue

In the preceding chapters we have touched on some vital Christian disciplines that will help you build your spiritual life from the inside out. Your growth will not come merely by reading the book or dabbling in the disciplines for a week. The disciplines presented must be established as regular habits in your life. Start with those you feel you need most and reserve time to study them and practice them daily.

The classic phrase "I don't have time" is not a valid excuse. We all find time for the things we deem most important in our lives. Great spiritual leaders in biblical record and church history found time to build their relationships with God. Spiritual growth is hard work, lonely work, and questioning work. We are all tempted to seek the quick, easy spiritual fix today. The twist of the TV dial to a religious program, a couple of hours at church, a quick glance at our daily devotional booklet and we feel equipped to face the battles of our day. A skimpy diet of spiritual K-rations can only leave us suffering from spiritual malnutrition. It is little wonder that today's Christian is battered into submission to secular pressures long before next Sunday's doxology is sung.

You will not be ready to face the challenges of this book until you realize that *you* are responsible for your own spiritual growth. You are the one who must do your own spiritual homework for the rest of your Christian journey on this earth. The Bible encourages us to grow up in Christ. The process of growth is the personal responsibility of each of us. We either choose to grow or remain as we are. Consistent growth means consistent living. What others around you are doing or not doing is not your primary concern. Your spiritual growth is your first order of business and primary concern.

I spent many years in my own Christian journey hoping to hear the right speaker at the right time or read the right book that I needed. When nothing seemed to click and I wasn't growing, I easily placed the blame on others. I joined the host of disgruntled church members who point accusing fingers at their pastor and state that they are not being fed.

It is time we quit perpetuating the model of the spoon-fed Christian and teach one another how to be responsible for our own spiritual growth. We must learn once and for all to walk the narrow, quiet, disciplined walk with God.

What ever happened to ordinary Christians? They never really left. They just got engulfed by the big Christian program machine. Many of them are breaking free, getting their priorities realigned, and beginning to walk in the way of the Spirit.

This book is the beginning of your challenge to grow. You probably feel like Gideon who said: " 'O my Lord, how can I save Israel? Indeed my clan is the weakest in Manasseh, and I am the least in my father's house.' And the Lord said to him, 'I will be with you and you shall defeat the Midianites as one man' " (Judges 6:15, 16, NKJV). Gideon pleaded his case for being very ordinary. Perhaps he thought his ordinariness would get him off the leadership hook. God's comeback was simply "I will be with you and you will win."

God uses ordinary Christians who accept their strengths and weaknesses and choose to live their lives from the inside out by building Christian disciplines. May your journey be more successful from reading this book!

Notes

Chapter One

1. Funk and Wagnall's Dictionary

Chapter Three

1. Francis MacNutt, *The Prayer That Heals* (Ave Maria Press, 1981), p. 13.
2. O. Hallesby, *Prayer* (Augsburg Press, 1931), p. 68.
3. MacNutt, *The Prayer That Heals*, p. 10.
4. MacNutt, *The Prayer That Heals*, p. 12.
5. Emilie Griffin, *Clinging* (Harper and Row, 1984), p. 41.

Chapter Four

1. Urban T. Holmes, *Spirituality for Ministry* (Harper and Row, 1982), p. 18.
2. Holmes, *Spirituality for Ministry*, p. 184.
3. Tilden Edwards, *Spiritual Friend* (Paulist Press, 1980), p. 126.
4. Alan Jones, *Exploring Spiritual Direction: An Essay on Christian Friendship* (Seabury Press, 1982), pp. 77–79.
5. Holmes, *Spirituality for Ministry*, p. 189.
6. Holmes, *Spirituality for Ministry*, p. 190.

Chapter Five

1. Elton Trueblood, *The Incendiary Fellowship* (Harper and Row, 1967), p. 43.
2. James Fenhagen, *More Than Wanderers* (Seabury Press, 1978), p. 3.

Chapter Eight

1. Albert Edward Day
2. Albert Edward Day
3. Susan Muto, *Pathways of Spiritual Living* (Image Books, 1984).

4. Richard Foster, *Celebration of Discipline* (Harper and Row, 1978), p. 1.
5. Hallesby, *Prayer*, pp. 12, 13.
6. Muto, *Pathways of Spiritual Living*, p. 121.
7. Henri Nouwen, *The Way of the Heart* (Seabury Press, 1981), p. 35.
8. Muto, *Pathways of Spiritual Living*, p. 56.
9. Henri Nouwen, *Making All Things New* (Harper and Row, 1981), p. 68.
10. Basil Pennington, *A Place Apart* (Image Books, 1985), p. 34.
11. Campbell McAlpine, *Alone with God* (Bethany Publishers, 1981), p. 7.
12. Muto, *Pathways of Spiritual Living*, p. 88.
13. Foster, *Celebration of Discipline*, p. 42.
14. Foster, *Celebration of Discipline*, p. 52, 53.
15. Thomas Merton, *What Is Contemplation?* (Templegate Publishers, 1978), p. 41.
16. Merton, *What Is Contemplation?* p. 26.
17. Gordon MacDonald, *Restoring Your Spiritual Passion* (Oliver Nelson, 1986), p. 218.
18. Muto, *Pathways of Spiritual Living*, p. 74.
19. Muto, *Pathways of Spiritual Living*, p. 174.
20. Foster, *Celebration of Discipline*, p. 122.
21. St. Teresa of Avila, *The Interior Castle* (Paulist Press, 1979).

Chapter Nine

1. Henri Nouwen, *The Wounded Healer* (Image Books, 1972), p. 94.
2. Nouwen, *Making All Things New*, p. 90.

Chapter Ten

1. Alan Jones, *Soulmaking* (Harper and Row, 1985), p. 6.
2. Muto, *Pathways of Spiritual Living*, p. 43.
3. Jones, *Soulmaking*, p. 22.
4. Thomas Merton.

5. Muto, *Pathways of Spiritual Living*, p. 47.
6. Jamie Buckingham, *A Way Through the Wilderness* (Chosen Books, 1983), p. 53.
7. Buckingham, *A Way Through the Wilderness*, p. 141.

Chapter Thirteen

1. Susan Muto, *Pathways of Spiritual Living*.
2. Brother Lawrence, *Practicing His Presence* (Christian Books, 1973), p. 42.
3. Lawrence, *Practicing His Presence*, p. 42.
4. Lawrence, *Practicing His Presence*, p. 73.

Chapter Fourteen

1. C. Peter Wagner, *Your Spiritual Gifts Can Help Your Church Grow* (Glendale, CA: Regal Books, 1978), p. 42.

Chapter Fifteen

1. A.B. Simpson (hymn)

Bibliography and Suggested Additional Reading

Pathways of Spiritual Living, Susan Muto, Image Books, 1984
**Meditation in Motion*, Susan Muto, Image Books, 1986
Alone With God, Campbell McAlpine, Bethany Publishers, 1981
**Hidden in Plain Sight*, Avery Brooke, The Upper Room, 1978
Making All Things New, Henri Nouwen, Harper and Row, 1981
The Way of the Heart, Henri Nouwen, Seabury Press, 1981
A Place Apart, Basil Pennington, Image Books, 1985
Celebration of Discipline, Richard Foster, Harper and Row, 1978
Prayer, O. Hallesby, Augsburg Press, 1931
**Teach Us to Pray*; Andre Louf; Darton, Longmon & Todd Pub., 1974
What Is Contemplation?, Thomas Merton, Templegate Publishers, 1978
**Seeds of Contemplation*, Thomas Merton, Anthony Clarke Pub., 1961
More Than Wanderers, James Fenhagen, Seabury Press, 1978
**A Guide to Prayer for Ministers and Other Servants*, The Upper Room, 1983

---

*books *not* quoted from in mss.